Routledge Revivals

I0130867

Psyche's Lamp

Psyche's Lamp
A Revaluation of Pyschological Principles as Foundation of all thought

by
Robert Briffault

Routledge
Taylor & Francis Group

First published in 1921 by George Allen & Unwin Ltd

This edition first published in 2018 by Routledge
2 Park Square, Milton Park, Abingdon, Oxon, OX14 4RN
and by Routledge
52 Vanderbilt Avenue, New York, NY 10017, USA

Routledge is an imprint of the Taylor & Francis Group, an informa business

© 1921 Taylor & Francis

Publisher's Note
The publisher has gone to great lengths to ensure the quality of this reprint but points out that some imperfections in the original copies may be apparent.

Disclaimer
The publisher has made every effort to trace copyright holders and welcomes correspondence from those they have been unable to contact.
A Library of Congress record exists under ISBN:

ISBN 13: 978-0-367-11113-7 (hbk)
ISBN 13: 978-0-367-11114-4 (pbk)
ISBN 13: 978-0-429-02489-4 (ebk)

PSYCHE'S LAMP

PSYCHE'S LAMP

A REVALUATION OF PYSCHOLOGICAL
PRINCIPLES AS FOUNDATION
OF ALL THOUGHT

BY

ROBERT BRIFFAULT

LONDON: GEORGE ALLEN & UNWIN LTD.
RUSKIN HOUSE, 40 MUSEUM STREET, W.C.1
NEW YORK: THE MACMILLAN COMPANY

First published in 1921

CONTENTS

PSYCHE'S LAMP

INTRODUCTION

At a time when so much in our estimates, conceptions, opinions, calls for fundamental reconsideration we are reminded that all thought and discussion, to whatever aspect of confronting problems, social, political, ethical, vital and personal, they may be directed, posit psychological premisses. Every exploration of the stream of human affairs leads us to its fountain-head, the soul of man ; and it is upon our view of its nature and operation that all our evaluations must finally rest. European thought, on emerging from the quaint rectilinear rigidities of scholasticism, was compelled to regard epistemology, the theory of cognition, as the propædeutic to all other thought. But far more is involved in the questions that press upon the modern mind than mere speculative curiosity ; and it is not our view of the operation of our cognitive powers alone, but of the springs and determinants of all action and of all thought, of all desire and endeavour, which, it is borne in upon us, is implicit in all our judgments. In the darkness and confusion of a human world under reconstruction, where immemorial landmarks lie strewn and buried under the debris of collapsed superstructures, we shall vainly endeavour to thread our way to any purpose unless we can pierce the obscurity by the light of Psyche's lamp.

It is in some measure from a sense of that need that reflective persons are drawn with renewed interest to psychological problems, and that many who are unaddicted to the sciences and to whom the very uncouthness of their language is repellent are disposed to relent from that attitude in favour of the science of the soul.

The zeal of those enthusiastic inquirers meets, I fear, with much discouragement and disappointment. Their reports are in general most disconcerting. I have heard some declare that there is no such thing as a science of psychology ; that one might reach deep enough in the study of its accredited textbooks and ·find little ; and concerning such fragmentary and conflicting views as are current they recalled the saying of Xenophanes, ' δόκος δ'ἐπὶ πᾶσι τέτυκται '—opinion, ' doxy,' is over all.

The fact is that psychology is not an organized science. Any department of inquiry becomes an organized science only under the unifying and vitalizing influence of some principle of interpretation which touches its basic conceptions and informs each isolated fact with a significance that knits it with all others into an organic whole. And, since primitively the human mind leaves no blanks in its scheme of things, any such basic interpretation can only be attained by violently displacing principles and conceptions previously accredited. Thus astronomy first became an organized science by the overthrow of the geocentric system and the enunciation of the Keplerian laws ; dynamics arose from the downfall of the Aristotelian dogma of motion and the formulation of the laws of Galilei ; chemistry with Lavoisier's exposure of the doctrine of phlogistic substance and his explanation of oxydation. Biology came into being by the collapse of the dogma of creation ; though, failing a consistent view of the mode of operation of evolution, it remains in the Copernican, and has not yet reached the Keplerian phase of development. Physiology and psychology have not yet become organized sciences at all. They are merely aggregates of disjointed theories and observations which, however valuable in themselves, afford no view of the general character of the phenomena which they investigate.

Is it mere coincidence that the natural sciences have developed in the order of the remoteness of their subject-matter from the centre of human interest, and therefore of human prejudice, from man himself ; first conquering the distant stars, then the physical world, then the world of organic life, and remaining at last held up by the problems of man himself, his organism, his soul ? Is it the intrinsic difficulty of the task or the force of established prejudice which constitutes the increasing obstacle ?

There have been controversies in abundance, but no revolutions in the realm of psychological science ; no hieratic myth, no geocentric theory or doctrine of creation, has been finally relegated to limbo. Paralogisms such, to take but one instance, as ' the unity of the Ego,' which was reduced to tatters over a century ago by the critique of Kant, recur serenely as the *leit-motiv* of official teaching in our great English universities in the present year of grace. Is it plausible to suppose that while in every other science progress has only been possible by the sweeping away of primitive conceptions, here alone, of all domains of knowledge, the human intellect has from the first seized the outlines of truth so infallibly that no occasion could arise to alter them ? When we consider the genesis of psychological science from theological ontology and scholastic epistemology, the academic seclusion in which she has long been nurtured, in close association with her confederate, the official Science of Virtue, it may be suspected that in even greater measure than in other fields of enquiry, the obstacles in her path are not merely the rocks and natural accidents of the ground, but walls and fences and artificial rockeries raised by pious hands. And it can cause us little surprise that the science of the soul has in general picked her steps amid those venerable impediments with beseeming caution and delicacy.

The methodical psychologist meets with his first perplexity as soon as he attempts to define the province of his science. To define the 'province' of a science is not 'a matter of very vital importance; for knowledge is essentially one, and every aspect and portion of it interweaves with, and bears upon, all others; such arbitrary subdivisions as we may choose to establish being essentially devices of systematic convenience. One would think to hear some speak that a science is a sort of Imperialistic State, the frontiers of which must needs be diplomatically delimitated on the map of knowledge, or that it is some game of ball, of which the rules are to be laid down in detail and honourably observed. One psychologist says to another, 'That is not psychology,' much as one might say, 'You're not playing the game; that isn't cricket.' A quite abnormal degree of importance attaches here to this business of defining the right and proper sphere of the science, an importance arising out of the questionable situation of psychology on the border-land of what are traditionally regarded as two wholly disparate spheres of human knowledge—the physical and the metaphysical. That division itself, the expression of a metaphysical dogma, is, I venture to consider, of no more essential significance than any other subdivision of human enquiry. The repudiation of metaphysics, whether in science or in life, can never mean anything else than the assumption of inconsidered, and therefore fantastically false, metaphysics. Physical science, coming as she does at every turn in contact with metaphysical questions, is like all other sciences, compelled to posit metaphysical postulates. Newton himself—for all his ' hypotheses non fingo '—teems with metaphysical doctrine; and modern physics is three parts metaphysical.

In the physical sciences the pretence of eluding metaphysical questions may, however, be plausibly enough maintained, for their outlook is sufficiently characterized by the forms of physical experience. But when psychology, ambitious of following the example, likewise protests her unconcern with ontology, the profession is not at all so easy, is in fact desperately impracticable. For the very enterprise upon which she is embarked, the exploration of the inner world of mind, posits a stupendous ontological dogma, namely, that there is a distinct and self-contained world of mind separated from all else by the unbridgeable abyss of substantial disparity, and coextensive with conscious experience.

That dogma, it is to be noted, did not in the first instance arise full-blown out of the epistemological grounds on which it has since come to rely for its justification. Long before the latter became susceptible of distinct enunciation the notion of the soul as a double of the living body, suggested chiefly by dream experience, had become immemorially established in primitive human thought. The doctrine of substantial dissimilarity, elaborated in Neoplatonic theosophy and Patristic theology, was first set forth with uncompromising emphasis by Descartes, the first writer who, in modern Europe, may be said to have initiated a separate science of psychology. When it is realized that no man has the remotest conception of what a ' substance ' is, we may estimate the audacity of laying down the existence of *two* distinct substances differing in their essential nature, that is, in that about which we know absolutely nothing. The dogmatism of Descartes's procedure is displayed in the anticlimax which it reached in his solution of the consequent question, ' Where should the distinct substance of mind be considered to begin ? ' For he pronounced all animals, and likewise the human organism and its functions, to be purely ' automatic,' that is, effects of the mechanical forces of the physical world ; the unique substance, mind or soul, being confined to a minute portion of the human body, namely, the pineal gland. That conclusion of the founder of the dualistic theory evinces a misconception of the very grounds that may be advanced in its defence, as ludicrous as that of the innocents who in the last century professed to evolve feeling out of the movements of molecules.

Those grounds of distinction are epistemological, that is, they are purely psychological.

Epistemologically the inner world of mind ' contains ' the entire universe. Orion and the Pleiades, sun-drifts and nebulæ, the globe, its hills and oceans, beasts and birds, men and women, are, in so far as *known*, but parts, feelings of the knowing mind, which by no possibility can reach beyond its feelings. But that upsetting and irrefutable demonstration which staggers and perplexes the ' plain man,' seeming to dissolve the solid world into such stuff as dreams are made on, leaves, as a matter of fact, things exactly as they were before. For in that universe of feelings ' contained ' within consciousness we come anew upon the self-same relations and distinctions between our feeling organism and the stars, ourselves and our dinner, ourselves and the men and women about us, as in the world of unsophisticated experience. Nothing in it is changed by the Berkeleyan poser, which amounts to saying that we only know things by having a knowledge of them. What that ' knowing ' is, is the real question.

Consciousness is feeling ; and we can know, be aware of, conscious of, nothing but our own feelings. But feelings have developed the peculiar property of being *presentative*, of representing, that is, something other than the experienced feeling itself. Every feeling can be converted into an object of presentation by thinking about it ; our anger of an hour ago, our toothache of last month, our sorrow, can be contemplated. Our feeling in so doing is no longer anger, toothache, or sorrow, but the presentation of those feelings. And the feelings thus presented, or represented, can only be feelings of which we ourselves have already had experience ; we can only present to ourselves our own feelings.

Some feelings have, however, in relation to the urging needs of life, become presentative in a special manner ;

and the object of their presentation is what we call
' matter.' We shall see that those sensory feelings have
been differentiated by degrees out of the original, primitive
feelings of pleasantness and unpleasantness ; and not all
sensory feelings are to the same degree differentiated,
nor do they all supply the elements of our perception
of matter. A world, for instance, that should present
no sensory feelings but those of smell, of warmth, of
formless colour, would not furnish the notion of matter,
would be purely solipsistic. In their fully developed
form those sensory feelings constitute our knowledge of
matter. ' Knowledge '—that can obviously never be the
thing itself ; my presentation of last month's toothache
is not my toothache, even though the object of presentation is here a feeling which I have experienced, and the
presentation of it as close a copy, presumably, of the
original as a presentation can be ; it is a rehearsal, a
reproduction of the same affective attitude. But what
does the presentation of matter reproduce or rehearse ?

To reproduce my own experienced feelings is a fairly
intelligible performance ; the object of presentation is
a former attitude of the mind, and all that is required
is to assume the same or a similar attitude. But to
present, to picture something which is not my feelings,
something quite different from my feelings, is a feat of
intuition which could only be regarded as an inscrutable
and unintelligible miracle. That, of course, is no bar
to our recognizing the miracle in a world where much
is inscrutable and unintelligible. But, in fact, that
incongruous miracle does not happen. The perception
of matter is not at all an intuition of something different
from our feelings : it is, just as much as our presentation
of toothache or anger, a presentation in terms of our
feelings. What those sensory feelings which supply the
perception of matter present is a perfectly definite thing,
it is the representation of our potential actions ; that
and nothing else. Matter, its spacial extension and

relations, its form, resistance, consistency and texture, as presented by tactile exploration and manipulation, molar directed movements, and their synthesis in visual perception, represents the possibilities of our activity in the ambient in which we move. That ambient is ' external ' precisely because we can act upon it ; and the ' object of presentation ' is nothing else than the object of action, and the form of its presentation that of possible action.

Look at the starry heavens, the sea, the earth, the living bodies upon it ; does that sensory spectacle of solid substantiality convey to you any information beyond the variety of actions which, disporting yourself in it, and manipulating it, you could in thought perform ? There are, to be sure, certain superadded features in it, colours, odours, sounds, temperatures, which do not represent your molar action ; but those features, which in other ways serve the purpose of guiding action, do not enter into your perception of material substantiality, and need not therefore concern us here. The very fact that they are discarded and set aside as irrelevant in our concept of matter should in itself somewhat pointedly indicate the nature of that concept ; it is entirely made up of the projection of our active movements, it *presents* nothing else.

' Knowledge ' of matter in terms of our motor activities is perfectly correct, reliable, and complete. Let us get rid of the superstition that there is anything illusory or deceptive about it. The accuracy of our presentation of matter is the most readily and the most constantly verifiable knowledge we possess. That log of wood which appears to me as distant so many paces, of a certain size and form, of a certain rigidity and texture, is exactly what it appears to be ; every one of those impressions I can verify by going up to it, handling it, operating on it. Sensation may under certain circumstances be deceptive, as when I mistake a flat painted surface, or a reflection, for a solid body, or estimate the size of the moon as less than that of the Peloponnese; those are illusions *because* subsequent activity will not be consistent with those presentations formed from inadequate experience. But there is no illusion whatever in the normal presentation of matter, for it quite accurately represents everything which it professes to represent.[1]

Illusion, deception, are only introduced by theoretical thought when it conceives that the presentation of possible action represents anything else, that sensory knowledge of matter is I know not what inconceivable 'reflection' or 'picture' of its 'being' or 'substance.' That is gross, glaring fallacy and absurdity, but it is not sensory perception, but metaphysical misthought that is responsible for it. And that absurdity of thought is exposed by thought in the flat self-contradiction of a substance which exists independently, that is, apart from our feelings, and the attributes of whose existence yet consist solely in feelable characters. It is the essence of the concept of 'substance' to be what it is *independently* of any relation to anything else,[2] while it is the essence of matter that all its characters depend upon our feeling it. No two concepts could stand in more radical opposition to one another; and no contradiction could be more absolute than the identification of the two.

---

[1] Any understanding of matter was absolutely impossible for faculty-psychology, and is so, so long as sensation is regarded as 'given.' "The senses do not deceive because they do not judge," said Kant. On the contrary, they *do* judge, but that judgment is entirely one of possible action.

[2] "τὸ πρώτως ὄν, καὶ ἁπλῶς ὄν."
Aristotle, Metaphys. vii, c, i.
"Substantia est ens tanquam per se habens esse."
Aquinas, De Potentia, a, vii.
"Res cujus naturæ debetur non esse in alio."
Aquinas, Quodlibet, ix, a, v ad 2.
"Substance is a thing which exists of itself in such manner that it needs for its existence no other thing."
Descartes, Princip. Philosoph. I, n. 51.

As soon as we think of matter not as an object of
action, but as a *source* of action, not as acted upon, but
as an agent, we leave entirely behind us the domain of
sensory presentation.

Sensory experience presents in addition to matter
itself the movements of matter, that is, the changes
which continually take place in the field of our possible
actions. Our own activity consists in nothing else than
in producing such changes in the material field. The
activity of matter, then, is of precisely the same character
as our own activity which the presentation of matter
delineates in its potential form ; both ourselves and
matter are sources of activity.

The way in which we ourselves come to act, to produce
changes in matter, is very varied and complex. It is
in fact the study and elucidation of that process which
constitutes the whole subject-matter of the science of
psychology. And there is here a radical difficulty which
is a fertile source of perplexity and confusion. Our
activity is not directly represented in our consciousness.
We can have presentations of our actions and of their
effects in the material world in just the same manner as
we can witness any other material changes, we can have
presentations of possible or of intended actions, we desire
certain objects, we have various sensations of muscular
effort, feelings of hesitation and of conflicting motives,
of resolution and decision, but our acts themselves are
not feelings and cannot be represented as feelings.
Feelings are in fact, as we shall see, the very converse
of our activity, they are actions upon us, and cannot
therefore possibly represent our own actions. Our actions
are material, they are performed by our material bodies
on material objects ; and it is here precisely that the
gap occurs which puzzles and perplexes us, the gap
between our idea of moving our arm and the actual movement of our arm. We are at a loss to conceive how the
one can be ' translated,' as we say, into the other. The

cause of action cannot be presented in terms of matter, which is the object of action, or in terms of feeling, which is the effect of action; hence our total incapacity of forming any presentation of a *primum mobile.* We give various names to the cause of activity, such as force, power, will, energy, and the like, but those words do not stand for any clear presentation whether in terms of matter or of feeling.

But, although we have no feeling of action, *all* our feelings are in one way or in another intimately connected with our actions; and we regard ourselves as agents, we have the general sense of activity, not because we have any feeling of agency, but because every feeling of ours is directly related to our acting, and has no significance apart from it. And thus it is that in spite of the absence of any presentation of activity, the cause of activity is conceived, however vaguely and inconsistently, in terms of our feelings. And indeed we cannot do otherwise; for all presentations whatsoever are and must needs be in terms of our own feelings, even sensory presentations being in reality nothing else but representations of our own feelings. Accordingly, when we think of matter as a source of action we are thrown back on a presentative analogy of our own feelings.

The physicist in his investigation of physical phenomena aims at inquiring not only into our possible action upon things, but into the causes of the actions, the movements of things. This he can to some extent accomplish in two ways, either by linking up things into larger systems by means of ' laws ' or by an ' ether,' or by decomposing things into smaller and smaller constituents, into molecules and atoms, and thus explaining the total resultant action of things in terms of the movements of their component parts—as ' forms of motion.' But, having subdivided things into parts, he is inevitably brought at last, if he desires to go farther into the explanation of actions, to a conceptual presentation which is no longer in terms of sensation, that is, of our action upon things, but in terms, darkly and vaguely, of our pure feelings. To the physicist the ultimate source of motion is, it is true, but a mathematical symbol, the value of which is the sum of effects ; but it can only be presented, thought of, as a presentation of feeling, just as our presentations of the feelings of other men and women can be nothing else than the presentation, by analogy, of our own feelings.

Men and women are sensorily presented to us as corporeal, material objects ; we also think of them by inference as having feelings similar to our own. If we imagine ourselves peering into the living structure of their organisms, of their brains, say, or of the cells of their brains, of the molecules and atoms of those cells, we are still regarding them in precisely the same way as when viewing the flesh of their limbs ; to peer into their anatomy can only assist us in explaining their actions by enabling us to discover in the movements of the constituent parts of their organisms the components of the total movements of those organisms ; but so far as perceiving anything else we are exactly as far advanced when viewing their skin as when viewing their cerebral molecules : we are perceiving them as stuff that we can manipulate. From the presentation of manipulatable stuff I cannot derive that of a feeling or that of a source of activity. But if we peer into living structure with the eye of the physicist, seeking the source of its activity, it is not upon molecules or atoms that we come, but upon something which, although it is not indeed feeling, is so intimately connected with it that it is constantly confused with it and represented in terms of feeling.

The science of psychology in its academical development, and likewise in the blind and futile revolt against it which arrayed itself in the incongruous garb of a quasi-physiological materialism, has built upon the quicksand of a metaphysical confusion of thought. And the consequences are not, as many have imagined, to be eluded by loudly repudiating all metaphysical responsibility, and by tossing over the problem of ' the relation between mind and matter ' to its inventor, the metaphysician. On the contrary, those consequences, like avenging furies, dog every step of the psychologist and pervade every portion of his insecure superstructure, which, while it lasts, is an enchanted castle fatally unamenable to any interpretative effort, and which must at last come tumbling about his ears in the utter ruin of irreconcilable antinomies. For as long as it remains a ' separate ' and self-contained universe no interpretation of any phenomenon within it is possible, unless it can prove itself to be indeed complete, and can discover within its own orbit the causes and the effects of its constituent elements ; and in proportion as the psychologist entrenches himself within a line of demarcation drawn with emphasized stringency, protesting that ' conscious experience ' alone is his concern, that ' psychology is introspection, and what is not introspection is not psychology,' do his difficulties grow more desperate. And whether that ' separate universe ' confesses to the scholastic impeachment of substantiality or no makes no essential difference ; it must share the fate of the dualistic fallacy, which is in reality a form of materialism, for it is from the substantiality of matter that the notion has been extended to mind, thus creating a second ' substance,' and the latter must inevitably be involved in the ruin of matter.

There is no such thing as a self-contained world of consciousness.

To epistemological psychology the mind naturally was a cognizing, knowing thing, the Nous, nay, a thinking thing—the *res cogitans* of Descartes ; the soul, or in more modern phraseology, the ' subject of experience,' was a spectator, and consciousness '*ein Schauspiel nur.*' It is a fact, which in our revolt against that paralytic view of mental life we are prone to minimize, that consciousness is overwhelmingly cognitive ; and the more elaborate its development, the more is its centre of focused distinctness occupied with presentations and with cognitive processes. It is not cognition alone, but the entire world of consciousness, which is functionally subordinate to the conative activities of the organism, to which every element of consciousness converges and of which it is an instrument and product. And that activity which constitutes the basis of all conscious phenomena, as of all life, is not itself an element of consciousness, is not represented in consciousness. To take a trivial everyday illustration, self-knowledge of our own individual ' character ' is not to be derived from any introspective experience, but from experience of our actual behaviour just as if we were dealing as an indifferent observer with the behaviour of some other individual. Consequently no science of introspective experience is possible ; for such a science would of necessity be compelled to limit itself to objects of which it must needs ignore both the causes and the effects as well as every link and connection between their constituent elements ; and those objects of investigation would therefore remain, in spite of any metaphysical disclaimer, as completely isolated as any scholastic ' substance ' or dualistic ' epiphenomenon,' and therefore destitute of any possible significance and for ever insusceptible of intelligible apprehension. Setting aside the linking of every mental process at either end through action and sensation with the material world, it is, on the contrary, impossible to investigate fundamentally any single event of conscious experience without the fact being revealed that nine parts of the process lie *outside* consciousness. Every fact of consciousness is but a detached and disconnected phrase torn from its context, and that context has to be sought elsewhere. Within the sphere of cogitation itself, the professedly characteristic sphere of the epistemologically conceived mind, the laws of the association of ideas by which it was once sought to connect the discontinuous elements of consciousness by an intelligible nexus, and thus to make experience a self-contained whole, are but superficial appearances of limited and questionable applicability. The elements of consciousness are only to a very small extent connected with one another ; it is in a sphere which is not that of conscious experience that the actual connection takes place. That supposed substantive and separate world of mind, of conscious experience, turns out to be but as the jagged crest of an iceberg the bulk of which lies submerged in a world which is not that of consciousness.

It is, in short, nothing less than the complete dissolution of the concept of mind which the science of mind is at the present day called upon to witness. Mind is consciousness, what is not consciousness is not mind ; yet the greater portion of mental processes lies outside the precincts of consciousness. Like her twin sister, matter, mind has become an untenable incongruity. Matter, that other child of primitive metaphysics, crumbles under the fingers of the physical inquirer. The physicist, however, is not pledged to save matter and cares little about its dissolution so long as he has definite dynamic energies to measure. But when the science of the soul also finds herself left with unconscious dynamic energies on her hands, either the definition of psychology or that of mind calls for radical reformulation.

Consider what distance we have travelled from the course laid down by scholastic psychology when a psychologist [1] quietly proposes to define the one-time science of mind as the Science of Behaviour. Behaviour ! Not ideas, not the soul, not the inner world, not that Cartesian substance secluded in splendid isolation within its corporeal tenement, is deemed the proper sphere of the science of mind, but the way people act, move their hands and feet, and what comes out of their mouths. In that conception of psychology a human being is placed

[1] Dr. W. McDougall.

under observation and his reactions studied in precisely the same manner as those of a metal or a gas.

That definition goes, to be sure, too far in the direction of objectivity. For it is the privilege of the psychologist to penetrate somewhat farther than the chemist or the physicist. He can not only note the nature of those reactions as they are actually seen in the behaviour of men and women under the eye of an observer, he can go behind the scenes and explore, at least a little way, the factors which modify and determine those reactions, a privilege which the chemist and the physicist do not .enjoy.

If a definition of the scope of psychological science be insisted on, it is as the Science of the Factors of Behaviour that it might most aptly be described. For those objects of consciousness, those presentations and ideas, those thoughts and those feelings of which consciousness is compacted, can no longer be regarded as the phantasmal objects of a contemplative vision, but are means and instruments whereby the quality of action is determined ; and that is their sole function. ' The mind,' consciousness, is no mere spectacle that can justify its existence by being simply viewed, but a link in the process of doing, a factor of action, one of the devices whereby through living beings changes are effected in the universe.

CHAPTER I

ACTION AND PURPOSE

LIFE, then, in us and in all beings, is manifested by actions. For each act, wise or foolish, that we perform we are in general able to adduce a rational justification by reference to an ulterior end, by showing, that is, that our action is a means to an end. The act is therefore described as purposive, and the end to which it is directed is called the purpose of the act. Most of our acts are thus referable to a proximate purpose, which again is conditioned by some ulterior purpose, that again by another, and so on. Our purposes, the justifications of our acts, are thus encased like a nest of Chinese boxes the one within the other. We dress that we may go out, we go out that we may be at a given place at a given time, we keep the appointment that we may advance some business upon which we are engaged, we are engaged upon it in order to earn money, we seek money in order to live, we live . . . Here we reach the last box of the Chinese puzzle. We wish to live, life is desirable ; that must serve as a sufficient reason. Or if we want to put a better face upon the matter, we may say that it is our duty to live, that for the sake of our family, for the sake of mankind, of some ideal or other, we are willing to bear the whips and scorns of time. But whether we aim high or low, in every such reference of our motives to some ulterior principle, we come at last upon a categorical end arbitrarily pronounced to be desirable. That ' ultimate purpose ' by which we justify our proxi-

mate and ulterior purposes stands itself in need of justification and, being ultimate, it is left unjustified. No
rational account of the goal of our acts is to be formulated ; for such a formulation would entail its conversion
into a means by reference to some object beyond it.
The concentric series upon which every act of our lives,
as a purposive act, rests, regresses to a purpose, the
purpose of which is not to be set down in thought.
To justify that end, to name the purpose which it
serves would be to give an answer to the last riddle of
things. No thinker, no system of metaphysics, no fancy
of mysticism or claim of revelation, has succeeded in
prefiguring, even darkly and dimly, such an end. All
our purposes are in the end purposeless.

The purposes which we formulate as rational justifications
of our actions are, then, of quite subsidiary import. They
do not represent the end of our actions, but merely various
steps which we adopt as means towards that end. What
we do is not to act in view of a given purpose, but to
discover the means of achieving something which we are
impelled to do. The impulse which prompts us to adopt
a particular purpose as a means to the satisfaction of
that impulse is the motive power that sets us, or any
organism, in motion. It is the impulse which determines
the purpose, not the purpose which determines the impulse.

We use the words ' purpose ' and ' motive ' as synonyms :
we say that a given purpose was the ' motive ' of such
and such an action. But a purpose is not a motive.
No human being was ever set in motion by a purpose.
You may conceive all the purposes you please, they will
not move you an inch unless you are impelled to make
use of them. The attribution of motive power to a
purpose—Aristotle's ' final cause '—is a flagitious misconception. Our actions are produced by the continued
operation of an efficient cause, the impulse that actuates
them ; the operation is only converted into an ' ideal
end ' by the introduction of means devised by the intellect

in the service of that operation, which thus becomes an intellectual category of finality by reference to those intellectual means. That finality is derived from the instrumentality, not from the active operation itself. Remove that use of means, and only the bare fact of action is left, divested of any ' final cause.' A purpose in view is only a particular device by which the efficient cause operates.

To have a formulated purpose in view is by no means a condition of action. It is only in difficult and unfamiliar circumstances that we devise means by the process of thought, and thus act with ' an end in view.' But that rational devising of means is but one of many ways in which the impulses of life operate ; it is a quite exceptional mode of behaviour. We do not go about life in that scheming, designing fashion ; we do not unpack our nest of Chinese boxes at every turn. That is an act of philosophy, not the ordinary procedure of life. The purposes of most of our acts are only consciously formulated as an afterthought. That formulation is a ratiocinative spelling backwards of the actual psychological process. It is an *a posteriori* psychological analysis, a post-mortem which we hold on our actions. Our intellectualistic analysis extends to all our acts a language derived from a very exceptional type of action ; and by calling the ways and means which we employ to satisfy the impulses that actuate us ' purposes,' we consider that our actions are thus rationally justified, and that we are actuated by purposes. That, of course, is the purest delusion.

To explain how our actions are brought about used to be thought a fairly simple matter. It was considered— and is even now considered by some writers who ought to know better—that the question is adequately elucidated by saying that we seek what gives us pleasure and shun what gives us pain, and that the motive force of our lives is to strive after happiness.

It appears incredible that anyone accustomed to clear thinking should ever have deluded himself into accepting such an answer, upon which, as the reader knows, whole systems of philosophy and even of politics have been founded. The pleasure-and-pain theory is merely a verbal roundabout : Why do we desire a given object ? Because it affords us satisfaction. Why does it afford us satisfaction ? Because we desire it. In the merry-go-round of such a vicious circle there is no getting farther. The formula leads us at once into desperate difficulties when we endeavour to discriminate between one order of actions and another. The hedonistic psychologist is at once held up by his old friend the martyr, and is eventually compelled to draw up a scale of pleasures and happinesses on grounds wholly extraneous to his theory ; for we have no means whatever of instituting a quantitative comparison between the pleasure of the sot and that of the saint—on the whole one would be inclined to consider the former's more massive.

The reason of those difficulties is that it is not the satisfaction which determines the desire, but the desire which determines the satisfaction. The pleasures and pains which we seek or shun are not attributes of given objects or situations, for the same object or situation will produce various and opposite feelings in different organisms, and in the same organism at different times. Those feelings depend on dispositions within ourselves which objects and situations affect favourably or unfavourably. Pleasure is the satisfaction of our impulses, pain is their thwarting. The pleasant or unpleasant quality of a feeling is the representation in our consciousness of the satisfaction or dissatisfaction of the impulses that actuate us. Various forms of satisfaction, that of the glutton and that of the hero, differ not because they weigh or measure more, but because they are the satisfaction of different impulses. And since all impulses tend towards their satisfaction, the pleasure-pain theory is a tautological truism.

It is extremely questionable, however, whether the formula is even true in its tautological sense. It arose as an *a priori* theoretical assumption rather than as a matter of psychological induction. Is it true that a feeling of pleasure is invariably attached to the acts or to the ideas of the acts which we are impelled to do ? Throughout organic life living beings are constantly submitting to all manner of pains and discomforts in their obstinate obedience to master-impulses, and it is very disputable whether in doing so any prospect or sense of greater pleasure or lessened pain enters into their conscious feelings at all. They will make excessive efforts and wade through jungles of discomfort in order to satisfy a quite moderate degree of hunger or appetite, altogether disproportionate to the heroisms manifested in indulging it. The reproductive instinct constantly chooses martyrdom with no prospect whatever of pleasure. Is the feeling of the hen-bird which turns against the dogs in defence of her brood one of pleasure ? No animal, in fact, and no human being spontaneously balances his profit and loss account. The true martyr and hero, like the invertebrate organism, does not feel at all in terms of pleasure and pain. The thinker who deliberately chooses poverty, bitterness, and the kicks of asses, in the service of odious and unpopular ideas knows quite well what he is about from the standpoint of the pleasure-and-pain balance-sheet. The appeal of strong or high impulses is quite independent of the physiological contrivance of pleasure and pain. The surrender to the imperative urge of a mastering impulse is accompanied by a feeling-tone, but even the non-thinker judges it to be an abuse of language to call that feeling pleasure. Consider the appeal from a purely affective point of view of all sad, melancholy, and even harrowing feelings and interests, provided they are on a high or a fundamental plane. The appeal of tragedy, for instance, has never been satisfactorily accounted for by the analysis of the pleasure-and-pain psychology. Pleasure and pain are primitive forms of feeling which serve their purpose of guidance in the more rudimentary, physiological stages of reaction ; in higher development and in connection with the more powerful, fundamental impulses they lose their importance and sink into comparative insignificance. The appeal of affective values is then sufficient in itself without assuming the primitive form of crude pleasure and pain. Where impulses are weak and hesitant, and therefore liable to be misled, they are guided by lively feelings of pleasure and pain, but where they are strong, reckless, ruthless, those leading-strings are superfluous, and are accordingly dispensed with.

The cause of our acting in a particular way is a disposition to act in that particular way. That explanation may sound unsatisfactory, and akin to that given by Molière's physician of the dormitive virtue of opium ; but it is the only one which we are entitled to give. We do not know the cause of our disposition to act, and where we cannot describe a thing by its causes we are compelled to describe it by its effects.

Ordinary human thought and the profoundest efforts of philosophers have always sought to disguise the crudity of that explanation. They have either tried to believe that we are actuated by ' purposes,' or by the quest of a certain thing called pleasure or happiness—notions which are quite erroneous and fallacious. Or they have given to our dispositions to act various names, such as the ' Will,' ' Will to power,' and the like. ' Will ' and ' power ' are words which simply mean a disposition to act. To call our disposition to act ' Will ' throws no more light on it than if we were to call it ' Tom ' ; and it has the disadvantage of suggesting misleading connotations.

The actions of living organisms are varied ; human beings differ widely in their behaviour from animals and from one another. Tastes differ, likes and dislikes differ. The conative dispositions manifested in behaviour appear to be greatly diversified.

Your own personal tastes are, I make no doubt, exquisite and refined. You are, we will suppose, keenly interested in art and in science ; you seek your truest pleasures in all that the human spirit has achieved of subtlest and of most precious and delicate. Those refined tastes of yours are, of course, the product of a certain education, of a certain culture ; your mind is trained to higher and more perfect pleasures, taps sources of interest and gladness that for the ignorant multitude are non-existent. In short, as you will readily admit, the tastes in the things you delight in and value are *acquired tastes*. The Philistine to whom they are caviare will pronounce them to be ' acquired tastes ' with a distinct note of disparagement in the expression. Those Pheidian marbles, say, the sight of which moves you with a strange thrill, that music that delights you, will cause neither pleasure nor pain to your greengrocer. He will probably prefer beer to Beethoven.

There are other tastes likewise, other likes and dislikes, other determinants of your actions, which, no less than your artistic or scientific tastes, are acquired. Your table-manners, for instance, your behaviour in social intercourse, the actions that derive from traditional and customary estimates and opinions, the whole beseemingness of your conduct and deportment, an enormous part of your morality, of your conscience. There are yet other and deeper dispositions which are equally, however anciently, in the stream of your heredity, acquired ; a host of instincts, like the instincts of animals, which are the product of a long evolution from primal protoplasm onwards ; primeval appetites and fears, ancient racial memories, the combativeness of remote male ancestors, the constructiveness of old builders, the sentiments of primitive worshippers, the gregariousness of antediluvian herds ; instincts which, down to physiological functional appetites, hark back to an immemorial ancestry, but which were, by that ancestry, acquired, the fruit of a long education by experience of the race. Those inherited instincts were originally no less acquired than your pleasure in Greek marbles or Tschaikowski symphonies. The fact is that all the forms of your conative dispositions, all your specific tendencies, likes and dislikes, are in their origin acquired characters. They are not original, innate and intrinsic characters of life, but products of development by experience. A specific appetence can arise in no other way.

A disposition to act can, in a living organism, become directed towards a definite object only as a result of experience of that object. You do not know whether you will like or dislike a thing until you have tried. You may, of course, by a broad induction describe the kinds of things or experiences you like and those you dislike. You may say, for instance, that you have a liking for literature or the drama ; but you must have read a particular book, seen a particular play, before you are in a position to say definitely whether you like them or no. The object of the reviews is to guide you as to the probability of your liking the book or the play sufficiently to justify you in spending your money on it. But the question can only be definitely settled by your reading or your hearing. Do you like Chinese music ? do you like Arabian poetry ? do you like the view from Corcovado ? The questions are absurd unless you have lived in China, studied Arabic, visited Rio.

We do not know what we like and what we dislike until we have tried ; we do not know whether a given object will satisfy or offend our conative dispositions, whether it will give us pleasure or pain. Hence comes about the ingenuous illusion that pleasure and pain are the determinants of our actions. The conative dispositions of living organisms must first have been tested by particular situations, by particular objects, before they can be known as pleasure or pain, appetence or averseness, before they can be established in the race as organized tendencies towards a certain form of satisfaction, a certain type of action. It is the process of experience, it is feeling and cognition with all their infinite variety which reveal the character of the conative dispositions of life, evolve them into specific desires, instincts, appetences, and bring about the correspondingly infinite variety of impulses into which the elemental dispositions of life become diversified.

Suppose that you are a chemist and that some entirely new mineral, a new element, which has been discovered in the bowels of the earth, is brought to you for the first time. You will set about investigating its properties; you will subject your new element to all manner of experiments, try the effects of heat, of electricity, of magnetism upon it, and of all the reagents and acids in your laboratory. The new element will behave in a definite way when subjected to each of those conditions, and you will be able to draw up an account of its various reactions, of the definite way in which it behaves in various circumstances. Although the mineral, which has slept for some billions of years in the depths of the earth, may never before have been subjected to such diversified treatment, been pounded in a mortar, had nitric acid poured over it, had evil-smelling sulphuretted hydrogen blown through it, been calcinated, magnetized, liquefied, gasified, its behaviour in each of those trying conditions is exactly determined by its constitution; every one of its reactions to a new condition reveals properties that lay latent in the disposition of its energy.

So it is with the dispositions that actuate living organisms. Life, we believe, is continuous from the first primordial protozoon to our own organism; at no time, if we allow the conception of organic evolution, has any new principle entered into it, been superadded to its disposition. Life reacts to experience, to feeling, to pleasure and pain ; but that reaction is determined by the conative disposition of which it is the expression in consciousness. As experience becomes diversified, so do the forms which the conative disposition of life assumes ; as experience expands, so does the scope of life's energies expand ; as feeling, cognition, develop, so do those energies attain to fuller, clearer expression of their direction and tendency. Anteriorly to experience they grope in a world unrealized, and no living being knows, we know not in our consciousness, what chord of feeling, pleasant or unpleasant, that experience will strike upon the dispositions of our being.

We have no knowledge, apart from experience, of the direction and tendency of the conative dispositions that actuate us. We do not know the law, so to speak, of our impulses. We are quite unable from any introspective knowledge to define the character, the ' whither ' of those dispositions. We are not in a position to answer off-hand the question, ' Whither do our desires tend ? '

Nothing surely, it would appear at first blush, is more vividly known to us than our desires, what we should like. If anyone were to request you to be good enough to draw out a little list of your desiderata, on the understanding that they would be duly fulfilled, you would certainly accept the task with considerable zest and enthusiasm ; and, whether you take an interest in psychology or no, you would think that the most delightful exercise ever devised in psycho-analysis. Your desires would come tumbling over one another—an income of a million or so, exuberant health and a long life, that house, that steam-yacht that you have had your eye upon, the love of that woman, freedom, leisure to enjoy it all, and so forth. No task would be easier, you think, than to express your desires.

But would it really be so easy ?

Mr. H. G. Wells has somewhere a story about a commonplace young man to whom was granted the gift of performing miracles, of realizing whatever came into his head. And the story of what he did with that priceless power is a tale of such absurd tomfoolery and senseless, dangerous pranks that even he, though below the average of stupidity, came to see the idiocy of it, and his utter unfitness, from the point of view of his own welfare, to be trusted with such a power ; and that he asked to be relieved of it. Mr. Wells's thaumaturgic young man was a particularly stupid specimen ; but most of us, I think, would experience considerable embarrassment in making use of omnipotence. How delightful it would be, you may have indulged in the day-dream after reading the *Arabian Nights*, to have the Slave of the Lamp make his bow before you and ask you to take the trouble to wish. One or two very simple wishes would probably occur to you at once, but you would very soon realize that any formulation of your wishes, to be at all consistent, and anything but grossly absurd, would require very careful consideration and deliberation, would indeed be not at all such an easy task as it seems, but a problem of considerable difficulty. We should, on consideration, if we had any discretion, probably end by asking our Slave of the Lamp to allow us a day or two to think the matter over carefully. Most of the things that it would naturally occur to us to wish for, wealth, health, long life, talent, are not ends in themselves, but merely means towards some object of appetence which we leave wholly undefined. We wish for Monte Cristo's millions, but what use we should make of them when we had them is quite another question. The scrambling *sacra fames* for wealth is mostly not an appetence at all for a positive object, but a negative desire to be relieved from the carking cares and abominable petty anxieties of non-wealth. I once came in a newspaper upon an account of a middle-aged couple somewhere in the United States who unexpectedly succeeded to millionaire wealth. This is the way in which they

3

employed the money : they had a palatial residence built, the greater part of which consisted in sumptuously appointed drinking saloons, where they invited their friends to come and get intoxicated at their expense ; when they went for a drive they were preceded by a brass band.

The pathetic impotence of our imagination whenever we endeavour to define or describe our heart's desire is vividly instanced in the utter and universal failure of all attempts to give any, even the most general, description of the delights of Paradise. Of the torments of Hell we have a multitude of detailed, vivid and entirely satisfactory descriptions, from those of the monk Tyndal and of Dante to the admirable manual published by Father Furniss for the use of young children, in which the boiling of the brain in the skull of an unbaptized infant, and the circulation of molten lead in the veins of unbelievers are minutely and convincingly described. But when it comes to picturing the condition of the souls of the blessed, the paralysis of our imagination is so complete, so pitiful, so manifest, that even the exponents of the happiness of the heavenly state who are most anxious to impress us with its surpassing desirability are driven to disown all attempts to formulate its nature, and to declare that the form and nature of that happiness is wholly inconceivable and indescribable, even in the most general terms.

We realize that a condition in which the desires that we can formulate should be completely satisfied would be a state of tedium and boredom before which the imagination recoils in horror. As a matter of fact, as we shall understand better by and by, such a state would not be merely one of boredom, it would be a state of unconsciousness. The Heaven of the Christian, perfect happiness, involves, no less than that of the Buddhist, as a psychological necessity the annihilation of consciousness. The condition of ' happiness ' is not the satisfaction of existing desires, but the progressive satisfaction of ever new desires. And the nearest possible approach within the limits of our experience to such a condition is not any perfected and rounded satisfaction, but the opportunity for the continuous exercise of our powers of self-development.

In nothing are we so completely powerless as in conceiving the tendency of our desires and appetites. The only desires that we are capable of conceiving are either for objects which have already been disclosed to us by our experience, or for the means towards some end which is left wholly undefined.

And yet it is clear that our wistfulness does not stop at the limit of the desires that we can formulate. It certainly reaches beyond them. There are in us wholly undeveloped capacities for joy. We all know the truth of the expression that there are times when ' we do not know what we want.' We are in a state of general dissatisfaction which we cannot specify, and for which we can suggest no remedy. We have come to a loose end. Maybe we shall have the good fortune to come upon an experience that will at once clear up the matter ; we shall have found the satisfaction of which we were unwittingly in search, and our soul cries ' Eureka.' But until that ' Eureka ' comes we are but thrusting out the pseudopods of our vain desires we know not whither. We are dull to perceive our soul's affinities ; experience must needs pound insistently at us to awaken them into consciousness.

. . . Conosceste i dubbiosi desiri ?

' Knew ye your dubious desires ? ' asks Dante of Francesca in that great poem of love's tragedy. Nothing is clearer than the goal to which the most potent motive impulse of living things is directed—the perpetuation of the race. But is that end even dimly present to the consciousness of the lover ? Is it present to consciousness in the effect upon us of wafted music, of blowing scents, in art, in poetry, which strike the chords of undefined emotions ?

The patent goal of the impulse which urges three-fourths of life is as unconscious as the most mechanical instinct which we count insentient and blind. And what is plainly manifest in that impulse which bestirs life to its fiercest activities is no less true of every end which under the illusory disguise of some short-reaching purpose we are driven to pursue. The ulterior ends, the goals, towards which our desires are but steps, remain hidden. Like the mason-wasp that stores food for the offspring of which she knows nothing, we are led to narrow desires by instincts to the end of which we are entirely blind. The inmost springs of our soul are unexpressed, unconscious and unknown.

The scope of that activity which is in us *conscious* is entirely confined to the sphere of means by which unformulated impulses strive towards realization in action. The source and the ultimate end of those actions are unrepresented in consciousness. The impulses which actuate our consciousness and our behaviour are as blind, as unconscious, as the instincts of the bee and of the wasp, as the ' mechanical ' forces of the inorganic world.

CHAPTER II

ORGANIC AND INORGANIC ACTION

To manifest itself in action is not a peculiarity distinctive of life ; it is a character common to all known existence. The whole universe is resolvable into motion, that is, into action ; it is dynamic, and no ' being,' no static existence, is discoverable. There is in this respect no distinction between the inorganic and the organic, the living and the non-living, the animate and the inanimate.

Those distinctions are not grossly apparent, and were not primitively drawn by human thought ; they are a matter of interpretation. Both the moon and my friend Jones appear to me as extended solid bodies which move ; I ascribe the movements of Jones to certain powers and dispositions which are not directly observable ; and I ascribe the movements of the moon likewise to certain powers and dispositions which are not directly observable. The movements of living objects, like those of inorganic objects, take place in relation to external conditions ; both are *reactions* to that relation.

It is not until we come to analyse the way in which organic and inorganic objects move that distinctive differences become apparent. Those differences are marked and manifest, so that scarcely any observer, whether scientific or no, ever commits the mistake of confounding a living with an inorganic object. But, strangely enough, when it comes to defining, or even roughly describing, those differences, human thought has invariably entered into a region of the utmost confusion, vagueness, and incongruity, substituting theories and interpretations of the causes of those differences for the observable facts. While primitively it failed to draw any clear distinction between the two kinds of reaction, it would appear to have become so impressed with the magnitude of the difference as to consider that it could only be accounted for by supposing it to be due to some totally different principle, which is the cause of the movements of living objects and which is entirely absent from inorganic objects. Indeed, some have thought one additional principle insufficient to account for the actions of living objects, and have accordingly postulated *two*, one to discharge their physiological functions and the other those of their consciousness, a vegetative soul or vital force, and a cogitative soul or mind. The supposition, once made, has given rise to a whole maze of new puzzles, as for instance : How does that entirely different principle postulated for the purpose of moving living objects come to perform—by a *generatio equivoca*—its function at all ; how do I come to move my arm ? " That I can stretch forth my hand at all," was to Carlyle " an inscrutable, God-revealing miracle." Can you form a clearer conception of why a stone falls to the ground ? Is there anything less mysterious in the one movement than in the other ? Of the two, the movements of my hand in relation to desires of which I am aware appear to me rather less mysterious than the movements of the stone in relation to nothing whatever of which I am aware.

Setting aside, however, for the present, all theories as to the causes of the differences between inorganic and living reactions, beyond the postulate that every reaction, whether inorganic or living, is the manifestation of a disposition to react in that particular way, let us consider the much more neglected question as to what those differences actually are.

The reactions of inorganic objects take place in a manner which is so rigidly invariable that it is mathematically calculable when the physical circumstances are known. The disposition to which each of those reactions is due is only manifested directly by the reaction itself, and never indirectly by other reactions which may be interpreted as modified manifestations of the same disposition tending to promote its operation. The stone tends to fall towards the centre of the earth, salt has an affinity for water ; but the only indications of those dispositions are the facts that stones do fall towards the centre of the earth, and that salt in the presence of moisture absorbs it. The stone does not circumvent obstacles in order to fall to the ground, salt does not seek water or in any way resist desiccation.

The reactions of living beings, on the other hand, are very much more variable than those of inorganic objects. They are only approximately predicable. Their disposition to react in given conditions in a certain way is, moreover, manifested not merely by the reaction itself, but by a series and variety of reactions which can be perceived to be conducive to the operation of that disposition and to the avoidance of conditions unfavourable to that operation. They seek and shun things by varied modifications of their reactions, they circumvent and overcome obstacles.

If I place a burning candle under a glass bell, its flame will gradually die out as the oxygen becomes exhausted or I pump it out. If instead of a candle I place a living creature under the bell, the same thing will happen. Both the flame of the candle and the flame of life require oxygen, and absorb it eagerly. But that need is, in the living organisms, manifested by other reactions besides the mere absorption of oxygen. Some organisms at the very bottom of the scale of life, the rotifer animalcules, will, when placed under the air-pump, take quite effectual steps to protect themselves. They will enclose themselves in a varnish-like substance which they secrete, and which enables them to retain a sufficient amount of oxygen and moisture to maintain their metabolism for a time. If I place a sparrow under the bell of the air-pump it will, as the supply of oxygen fails, show unmistakable signs of uneasiness ; it will make desperate, though ineffectual, efforts to get away, to get at the oxygen outside. If a trap-door be contrived in the bell of the air-pump, it may, in its indiscriminate efforts, hit upon the way of escape. A mouse under like circumstances will almost certainly succeed in finding its way to safety.

We cannot very well continue our investigation by placing a human being under the bell of our air-pump, but we can consider his behaviour in a quite similar situation. Suppose our human subject to be a passenger on an ocean steamer. Suddenly the steamer strikes a rock or an iceberg, and presently begins to settle at the bows. The event strongly affects the man just as the failure of oxygen affected the sparrow and the mouse ; but there is here this further difference : there is for the moment no actual failure of oxygen, but the man foresees that there is an imminent danger of a failure of oxygen, of asphyxia, of drowning. He forestalls the event, and he sets about taking various elaborate steps, such as helping to lower a boat, providing for a supply of food, keeping a look-out for a passing ship, setting up a signal, and so forth, to counter the menace.

The reactions of the candle-flame, of the living animals, of the man, are, ultimately analysed, manifestations of an appetence, need, or affinity for oxygen. But, while that need or appetence gives rise in the living beings to more or less elaborate, more or less effectual varieties of reactions, manifestly connected with that appetence, the flame of the candle combines with oxygen and dies as the supply of it fails, but does nothing else that is relevant.

The nature of that difference is the same whatever kind of organic or inorganic reaction we consider.

We are able to construct amazing machines which not

only serve a definite purpose, perform definite acts, but go through the successive steps of a complex performance in view of an ultimate result ; nay, which actually cope with the event of an occasional failure, adjust themselves to accidental circumstances. But there is no parallel between those machines—imagine them to be a thousand times more wonderful and efficient than they are—and an organic reaction. For all the purposes, however devious, which the machine fulfils are purposes which have been put into the structure of the machine by ourselves. They are not ulterior purposes of the machine, but of ourselves who made it. And however wonderful a machine may be, we can be quite sure that all the purposes it appears to manifest and the variety of situations with which it is capable of coping have, every one of them, been foreseen, not by the machine, but by the machine-maker ; and in so far as they represent means to ends, those ends are not at all those of the machine, but of the maker of the machine. A machine is merely a prolongation of human action.

So likewise the same distinctive difference between inorganic action and that of living organisms holds good of the most primitive and rudimentary acts of the latter as of the most elaborate, of any of those reactions in living organisms which we speak of as physiological as of the most acute or the most idealistic behaviour of a human being. In the crude example which we considered that character was exhibited in a much more marked and effectual form by the rotifer, a primitive unicellular organism corresponding to the cells which compose the organs of higher organisms, than by the bird or by the mammal.

Physiological science aims at explaining all the operations performed by the various organs and tissues of the body in terms of our knowledge of physical and chemical processes. All physiological explanation consists in such a subsumption, and to that aim and method is due the enormous extension in our knowledge of physiological function. But great as that development has been, and elaborate as are now our data concerning every observable physiological operation of the organism, it so happens that in no single instance has any physiological function been entirely reduced to terms of purely physical and chemical actions. Even simple processes which, on the face of them, seemed quite susceptible of a complete physical description, and were thought to have been so accounted for, are found on further investigation to involve factors not subsumable under ordinary physical laws. The ascent of sap in the vessels of plants, for instance, is seemingly quite intelligible by taking into account the suction produced by evaporation in the leaves, the pressure in turgid roots, and the capillary forces ; but it is found to be carried out mainly by contractions of the cell-walls of the vessels. Absorption through the walls of intestinal and other cells appears to be a straight-out case of osmosis through a membrane ; but the process is not governed by the laws of osmosis, but by a selective action exercised by each cell ; the cells are not fed, they feed themselves. No case of reduction of physiological function to physical terms has been discovered. That circumstance might, of course, be pure coincidence ; and we should have no right, considering the complexity of organic action, to taunt physiological science with the fact, and to say that because no physiological operation has been so analysed, it can therefore never be so analysed. But the position is somewhat different when we observe that the residuum of mechanically unexplained physiological action presents precisely that character which is peculiar to organic action and which distinguishes all the reactions of living things from those of inorganic objects.

We are not, then, to set down physiological action with mechanical action under one head, and ' mental ' action under another, but inorganic action under one, and both physiological and mental under another ; for there is precisely the same distinction between the physiological and the mechanical type as there is between the latter and the mental type of behaviour. So far as respects that distinction between mechanical and non-mechanical, the line of demarcation is not between mental and physiological, but between living and non-living ; and that other line of demarcation which we choose to draw between physiological performances, biochemical reactions, and conduct muscularly exteriorized, is quite arbitrary and unjustified by the facts. The one and the other order of reactions are distinguished from mechanical processes by the same differences.

Those differences are quite definite, but our ways of conceiving and describing them are not.

The description which first presents itself to our mind is to say that organic reactions are purposive, and inorganic reactions are not. When putting the matter in that way we are applying to all organic actions the terms of a very special form of our own action, and one, moreover, which we have interpreted inaccurately. We are not actuated by purposes, we are actuated by impulses. To have an ideal end in view is only one way, one very special method, of satisfying our impulses. We interpret by means of our intellect, and in doing so our intellect, which is itself an instrument of our impulses, imports into the interpretation its own mode of operation as an instrument, in the form of an ideal end. And the same intellectual operation will lead us to describe the reactions of the plant-cell of the protozoon as ‘ purposive,’ and will lead us to regard every efficient cause as a final cause. But that importation of our intellectual method into every mode of action is manifestly fallacious ; for what is meant by the purposive method is to have ‘ a purpose in view,’ and not only can we not suppose the plant-cell, the infusorian to have ‘ a purpose in view,’ but in the majority of our own actions we ourselves have no ‘ purpose in view.' And when we do, that purpose is not at all the efficient cause of our actions, but a very subsidiary mode of obtaining the means of satisfaction of impulses which have no ' purpose in view.' That extension of a concept derived from a special mode of action to all action leads inevitably to confusing inconsistencies. For it leads us to regard all those organic reactions which are exactly similar to those of our actions that make use of an intellectual purpose as ' purposive,' while we are at the same time compelled to declare that they have no purpose in view.

In order to express that peculiarly self-contradictory conception we have invented the words ' adaptation,' ' adapted,' ' adaptive.' Those words are an obvious subterfuge to shuffle out of the incongruous conception of a ' purposive ' action that has no purpose in view. They are, however regarded, ambiguous. We describe the actions of a living organism as being ' adapted.' ' Adapted ' to what ? ' To external circumstances ' is the usual answer. But ' adapted to external circumstances ' means nothing at all unless certain needs, requirements, interests, impulses of the organism which adapts itself, be postulated. The reactions of a living organism are not adapted to external circumstances only, but to the actuating impulses of the organism. What is called adaptation is the adjustment of the reaction of the organism to both terms, to the external circumstances and to its own impulse and disposition.

Animals occasionally act foolishly, and so do even human beings ; their actions are not adapted at all. The statement is therefore modified by saying that they are ' adaptive,' that they tend, albeit ineffectually, to become adapted. But some acts are not even adaptive—the flight of the moth into the flame, for instance, the roar of the hungry lion, the yapping of the terrier at a rabbit.

The fact is that the teleological character which we introduce into all our descriptions of organic reactions is not a fundamental, original and innate character of the reactions of life. It is true that an enormous majority of those reactions do manifest that relation of means to an end, and that numberless structural organs and complex functions are permanent and elaborate devices to promote by an intricate apparatus of means the ends of life in the individual and in the race. But those organs, those functions, and the whole teleological operation of organic reaction, are the result of a long process of development. That teleological operation is the effect of a much simpler mode of action out of which it has grown. That mode of action which characterizes organic as opposed to inorganic reactions is not the power of adaptation, but the power of *modification*.

If we study the behaviour of the simpler organisms we at once perceive that their power of adaptation simply means the power of *altering* their behaviour. If an infusorian freely swimming in a microscopic aquarium comes upon an obstacle, such as the glass wall of the vessel, it recedes and alters its direction by a small angle ; if once more it collides with the obstacle, its direction is again modified by a few degrees, until by successive repetitions of the process it comes to be reversed. Such a manœuvre is typical of the procedure of all organic reactions. It is what has been aptly called by Lloyd-Morgan the process of Trial and Error. If infusorians or other micro-organisms are placed on a glass plate the various parts of which are heated to varying degrees of temperature, the organisms will ultimately be found to be collected in that portion of the plate which offers the most suitable temperature for their development, the ' optimum temperature,' as it is called. That result is a definite adaptation, but if we observe the manner in which it is brought about we shall find that it is exactly similar to that followed by the infusorian when colliding with an obstacle. Each infusorian alters the direction of its motion whenever it passes from a more comfortable to a less comfortable temperature, until all are ultimately collected in the region of optimum temperature. There is, it may be urged, a certain amount of adaptive action in the fact that conditions which are injurious produce a reaction different from those which are favourable. But that distinction is, as we shall see, a necessary consequence of the variability of reaction, for injurious conditions cause a negative variation of those activities upon which they act injuriously, while favourable conditions stimulate them.

The teleological power of adaptability is, then, a derivative product of the more elementary power of modification. And it is this power of modifying their reactions which constitutes the essential distinction between the mode of action of living organisms and that of inorganic systems.

Now there is a very good reason why living organisms have the power of modifying their reactions and inorganic systems have not. In living organisms any reaction can be repeated over and over again by the same reacting system, while no reaction can ever be repeated a second time by the same inorganic system, for the latter is, so far as the particular reaction is concerned, completely destroyed by every reaction in which it takes part.

The cause of the actions of inorganic objects is not known. Scientists to-day call it ' energy.' That is only a word which means ' action,' or ' activity,' and adds nothing to our knowledge of the fact that all objects act and move. Since it is the ultimate fact of analysis, corresponding to the old categories of ' being ' or ' substance,' it cannot be explained in terms of an ulterior concept.

Although physical science cannot explain the nature of energy, it has demonstrated a very important fact concerning it, and illustrated some of the most abstract conceptions of Aristotelian metaphysics. Energy is a fixed quantity that can be measured. It can exist in a latent, potential state, and it can be liberated and act.

The expression 'potential energy' is, like much of the phraseology of science, highly disputable. Physical investigators have shed a flood of light on metaphysical conceptions while often displaying a pathetic simplicity in regard to metaphysical precision. 'Potential energy' is tantamount to 'inactive activity,' which is an absurd contradiction in terms. But 'potential energy' is, in fact, not inactive at all. It is abundantly employed in the maintenance of the configuration of the system which is supposed to 'contain' it in a latent state. Energy is 'stored' within a system by being employed in holding together the configuration, the form of that system. The 'potential energy' of a stone on a cliff, of a head of water, of a Leyden jar, of a complex molecule, is active in the stresses, masses, electric charges, chemical affinities, attractions, represented by the positional relation of the parts of those configurations. And those stresses, masses, etc., those apparently static qualities of material objects, are analysable into actual movements. The 'latent' or 'potential' state differs only from the active or 'kinetic' in that its operation is circumscribed within the limits of a system theoretically isolated from the rest of the universe. The energy which is potential in the lump of iron is kinetic in its molecules ; that which is potential in its molecules is kinetic in its atoms, and so forth. So that the opposition between potential and kinetic energy is only relative.

The concepts 'potential,' 'power,' 'disposition,' 'tendency,' etc.—to which may be added those represented by the words 'agent,' 'doer,' and the like—belong to the category of *form*. The energy of the physicist remains unchanging in quantity ; the manner in which that energy is distributed and circumscribed within a 'thing,' a given system of energy, a given 'agent,' is the form of that energy. It is that form alone which is significant, which constitutes differences, qualities. Energy, being regarded as a uniform unchanging quantity, can have no values because there are in it no differences. Destroy the form, you destroy the 'thing,' the object, the piece of coal, the molecule, the atom, and convert it into kinetic energy, into action. We can break up most objects into gaseous molecules; by more powerful agencies those molecules can in turn be broken up until nothing massive and formed remains. The energy which by its disposition constituted the system is redistributed into new configurations. The 'thing' is completely converted into action.

Whenever a configuration of potential energy is transformed into kinetic energy, that configuration is destroyed. Every system of energy which reacts comes to an end in that reaction; the reaction cannot be repeated by the same configuration. When a stone falls from a cliff, the configuration, stone-earth-ether, is destroyed. The reaction can only be repeated by building up the configuration anew, that is, by carrying the stone back to the top of the cliff. A configuration of energy does not, of course, correspond to what we call an object; the latter being a purely arbitrary delimitation effected in relation to our own uses and actions. The sun, the stars, which radiate heat and light into space, are thereby destroyed. We never twice see the same sun, the same star, but only what is left of them after each reaction in which the whole system giving rise to that reaction is consumed. In the machines which we make the energy is supplied by our winding them up, or providing them with fuel.

The same holds good of the chemical reactions of molecular systems. When a salt reacts with an acid, the salt and the acid are destroyed, and a new configuration is formed. Radium is destroyed by giving off energy and becoming converted into helium.

No inorganic system can react without its configuration, its form being destroyed by that reaction; and therefore no reaction can ever be repeated by the same configuration of energy, by the same 'agent.'

Those things which scientists speak of as electrons,

magnetons, atoms, molecules, multi-molecules, are systems of energy, of latent power. The simpler the constitution of those systems, the stronger the bonds by which the energy is tied within them ; the more complex the aggregate, the weaker the bonds, the more labile and unstable the configuration of energy. Simple substances, like hydrogen, are only broken up under very special conditions, as in the photosphere of the sun where the spectroscope shows us the presence of hydrogen resolved into single atoms, proto-hydrogen. ' Elements ' of complex structure, of high atomic weight, such as uranium, thorium, radium, are comparatively unstable, and are constantly being broken down with the release of energy. Still more complex aggregates, such as the relatively huge organic molecules, are in a state of unstable equilibrium, and readily become transformed, giving forth energy. Those substances called colloids are composed of a number of molecules loosely united into multi-molecules ; a portion of their energy is constantly and slowly active, and, owing to the extreme variety of affinities of the carbon atom, an enormous diversity of reactions and changes can proceed simultaneously within the system.

Regarded from a purely chemico-physical point of view, living systems of energy are colloids of the highest degree of complexity, instability and diversity of reactions. Those conditions give rise to entirely new possibilities. Their reactions consist, like all other chemical reactions, in the liberation of kinetic energy derived from the destruction of the internal configuration in which that energy was potential. But only a portion of the system is thus broken down in every reaction. The large reserves of energy which are maintained in those portions of the system which do not take direct part in the reaction are employed in simultaneous reactions. As a result of those correlated reactions the configuration destroyed by each reaction is built up anew from the reserve energy of the system, and from energy absorbed from the surrounding world ; the system of potential energy winds itself up as fast as it runs down ; it stokes itself, feeds. Thus the form, the configuration of the system, is maintained throughout the stream of changes. What cannot take place in any other physical or chemical system in the world can consequently take place here : a reaction can be *repeated* over and over again by the same configuration of energy.

From that circumstance momentous consequences follow. The configuration which is rebuilt after its destruction in a reaction is never exactly the same as it was before ; it is modified by the reaction. The second reaction will therefore differ from the first. If the first reaction has produced an effect favourable to the activity of the configuration of energy involved in that reaction, the subsequent reaction will be more powerful than the first. If, on the contrary, the effect of the first reaction has been unfavourable to the configuration which produced it, the activity of the latter will necessarily be diminished on a repetition of the reaction. By repetition of the process a continuous and increasing modification in the reaction takes place. The original reaction may become very much prompter and intensified, or it may disappear altogether. The system will not react as it did at first ; it will react in some other way. Its reaction has become *modified*. And by the elimination of reactions which lessen the power of the system to rebuild the destroyed configuration, its reaction will become *adapted*.

In our own experience the concomitant of a modification in our reactions is a *feeling*, a feeling of comfort or discomfort, of pleasure or pain. Feelings, pleasure and pain, do not cause us to act, they are not the motive power of our actions, but they cause us to *modify* our actions.

Human thought has for ages made a variety of suppositions to account for the differences in behaviour of living beings and inorganic objects. The most prevalent has been that of a separate principle, either confined to human beings (the soul), or common to all living things (the vital force). That solution by means of a special 'virtue,' or *deus ex machina*, is, of course, the easiest. It costs nothing ; and its value as an explanation is exactly proportional to its intellectual cost. But, directly connected with its complete impotence to explain anything, is the prolific power it possesses of bringing into existence teeming multitudes of insoluble riddles, incongruities and flat self-contradictions, so that a very large proportion of the pseudo-problems of metaphysics is the direct progeny of that felicitous solution. That unsatisfactory state of things has accordingly caused many at various times to put forward the opposite supposition, namely, that the cause of the actions of living beings, including men and women, is the same as the cause of the actions of inorganic objects.

That rival theory has assumed two main forms. Some, deluded by their opponents' own conception of matter, have professed to regard feelings as products or effects of the movements of material particles, much to the amusement of those who moved their arms by means of their thoughts. Some Greek thinkers, such as the philosophers of the Eleatic school, Parmenides, and later Empedocles, who lived at a time when epistemological distinctions were still somewhat hazy, and, accordingly, the Cartesian epistemological misconception of dualism had not yet brought confusion on human thought, also held the view that all activities, whether organic or inorganic, have a common cause. And in order to do so consistently, they and those who have followed them felt themselves compelled to assume that inorganic objects have feelings.

That assumption is not in accordance with our own psychological experience. For feeling in ourselves only accompanies a modification in our activity, and the activity of inorganic objects is never modified. We only experience a feeling when a change in the relation of our activities to those of the surrounding world calls for a change in our mode of action. Where no such change is called for, when our surroundings are perfectly ' normal ' and habitual, so that we react to them by well-established and unmodified reactions, those reactions take place without being accompanied by feeling, ' automatically ' and unconsciously. The principle of Hobbes, the ' Law of relativity,' as it is called, " *Idem semper sentire et non sentire ad idem recidunt*," is one of the best established principles of psychology. It has been disputed, by William James, for instance, who calls it a ' superstition,' and suggests that one might have the same old pain throughout eternity. The Christian Fathers were better psychologists ; they recognized the necessity of invoking a miracle in order to make possible the pains of eternal punishment. All feeling is a change from the normal equilibrium. When that equilibrium is disturbed two things may happen : the organism may adapt itself to the new conditions, or it may fail to adapt itself. In the first case those conditions become in turn ' normal ' and cease to exist as feeling ; in the second the feeling organism itself ceases to exist. Innumerable activities take place in us unaccompanied by any feeling so long as the conditions of their operation remain unchanged ; but let a change take place in those conditions of our physiological and automatic activity, and at once a lively feeling of discomfort is experienced.

Feeling is in ourselves entirely restricted to a very limited aspect of our activity. We have seen that neither the cause of our actions nor the end to which they are directed is represented in our consciousness. That consciousness is exclusively confined to the intervening process of employing means towards the satisfaction of the impulses which bring about our actions. ' Means,' ' purposes ' are nothing else than the cognitive method of modifying our reactions. That method constitutes an abbreviation of, and an improvement on, that of modification by trial and error under the guidance of pure feeling of comfort or discomfort. It is only in the face of a situation that is *new* that the operation of that intercalated process of instrumentality is called for. Consciousness, whether cognitive or affective, is only associated with such a change in the conditions of our activities as requires a modification of those activities. Where those conditions contain no element of novelty they are dealt with unconsciously and anæsthetically by the operation of our established reactions.

Suppose that we do assume that the cause of the activities of inorganic objects is exactly similar to that of our own, and that we can therefore analyse those actions psychologically on the analogy of our own feelings in just the same way as we analyse the behaviour of living things. If we apply the analogy accurately, we shall not be able to introduce any feeling into the transaction. For feeling does not exist in ourselves except as the concomitant of modification of reaction ; and no inorganic reaction ever is or ever can be modified, because the system of energy that gives rise to it is completely destroyed in the reaction itself. Feeling only occurs in the interval between the coming into operation of an unconscious latent impulse at the call of an occasion for that operation, and the consummation of that impulse ; in inorganic reactions there is no such interval. There is no interval between the operation of a cause, the contact of a reagent, for instance, and the effect or reaction which is brought about. There is no intercalated process between cause and effect ; there are no instrumental purposes, no means, in the operation of inorganic energy. Ascribe consciousness to the ' affinity ' of hydrogen for oxygen, conceive it to be a want, a desire, that consciousness will not come into being except in the presence of oxygen, and it will cease to be as the reaction is effected, that is to say, at the same moment. There is no reaction-time in inorganic processes ; where a reaction appears to occupy a certain time, that is merely due to its successive diffusion to various parts ;

the reaction is extended in space but not protended in time. In ourselves every conscious process is protended in time, it must last an *appreciable* time in order to be conscious at all. No conscious process known in our experience could take place under the conditions of inorganic reaction.

Those, then, who have supposed that if the cause of inorganic reactions is of the same nature as that of the reactions of living organisms, feeling must be postulated to be a concomitant of the former, were mistaken, and were misled by an insufficient knowledge of the conditions of our own psychic experience. On the analogy of our own psychology no such assumption is justified.

The movements of the inorganic world are said to ' obey ' certain physical and chemical ' laws.' The expression is, of course, highly metaphorical. What any scientist understands to-day by that expression is that the activities manifested by material bodies are observed to conform invariably to certain formulas which we have been able to induce from the observation of those activities, and which are, doubtless, partial aspects of wider uniformities. But when the phrase ' to obey a natural law ' first came into use in the seventeenth century it was intended to have a pious connotation. It was deliberately meant to suggest that material bodies actually ' obeyed ' a ' law ' imposed upon them by the fiat of an Almighty Creator. That ' obedience ' was supposed to convey a subtle implication of some sort of homage, of worship, of acknowledgment of supremacy offered by creation to its Maker. Conformity to natural law, that is, mechanism, was by our pious forefathers made a subject of religious edification ; that mode of interpretation being designed to rob the uniformity of mechanical processes of the lurking danger arising from the antithesis to the supernatural and miraculous. It was an animistic metaphor.

Instead of using that animistic metaphor, we might with equal propriety say that physical activities are manifestations of impulses to act in certain ways. The latter metaphor would be considerably more accurate as a statement of fact free from assumption ; for all that we directly know is that material objects act, and that activity can only be conceived as the manifestation of some inherent disposition to act. But a disposition to act does not imply feeling, which is only found in conjunction with the modification of action. No modification can take place in the activity of inorganic systems, which is arrested and at an end in the instant that their measured quantity of energy is balanced ; no reserve of energy can permit of persistence in the operation of the tendency. Only by the conative disposition of a living organism, which is not destroyed by its reaction, which renews itself, and can repeat, modify, its operation, can experience be accumulated and applied. In the delicate rhythmic equilibrium of that permanent instability of living matter were probably offered for the first time the necessary conditions of consciousness, the possibilities of feeling.

CHAPTER III

FEELING AND COGNITION

It is on presentations, sensory or conceptual, on thought, on cognitive objects and processes, that our consciousness is focused. But another form of conscious experience much more fundamental than cognition, though thrust by it into the penumbra of our consciousness, is invariably present—pure feeling, affective feeling.

There is no such thing as knowledge, as cognition pure and simple ; every cognition is embedded in a matrix of affective feeling. Whenever an object, an event, is present to the mind, through the senses or in thought, whenever it is cognized, there is much more in that experience than the mere fact of cognition, the mere fact that the object is apprehended as being such. You perceive a material object, say, to be big, hard, of a particular form and colour. Those features, whatever your theory of perception, whatever translation they may undergo in passing through your sensual means of investigation, are counted by you as characters of the object itself, characters of it, in truth, as the object of your action. But that object in addition strikes you as interesting or uninteresting, pleasant or unpleasant, beautiful or ugly ; it makes on you an impression over and above those features which you register as its characters. And, as a matter of fact, you will not trouble to note the first set of qualities at all distinctly and minutely unless the object first makes its appeal to you by virtue of some interest, of some use, of some pleasantness or danger, which in some way *affects* you, and directs your attention to it and to those descriptive characters which you note. The two sets of adjectives differ radically in their purport. The interestingness, the usefulness, the pleasantness, the beauty of the object are not regarded by you as intrinsic qualities of the object, like its shape and colour ; they are expressions of values which the object bears in relation to certain needs, desires, interests, tastes, likes and dislikes, which constitute your attitude towards it. The first set of qualities is cognitive, the second affective.

A fact is never merely registered, it commoves and colours our feelings. The experience which is utterly drab, trivial, blank and meaningless, is by that very insipidity framed in its particular feeling-tone.

The fact is disguised and obscured in the complexity of our experience. Countless sense-impressions pour in upon us every second, and we should in most instances be at a loss to assign an affective value to those experiences which seem to be thrust upon us without our asking.

> The eye it cannot choose but see,
> We cannot bid the ear be still,
> Our bodies feel where'er they be.
> Against or with our will.
> WORDSWORTH.

It appears to us that we are essentially experiencing, sentient beings continuously subjected from all quarters to a somewhat tedious bombardment of sensations, most of which are of little interest to us and have some trouble in attracting our attention at all, in making us observant. They are to us neither painful nor pleasant, beautiful or ugly. But the illusion—for such it is—of a bombardment by indifferent sensations is the effect of a highly elaborated development of sense organs which have become posted all about our organism to keep watch—not at all for purposes of idle curiosity, but in view of issues of life and death—over the environment. And, irrelevant as much of the information appears to be which those watchful sentinels transmit, we, as a matter of fact, only take account of just those sensory data which, in respect of some vital interest or present purpose, are significant. In order to engage our attention at all, in order to be perceived, they must possess that affective value, a relation of some kind to what, for the present, we deem our interest. No sensation enters our consciousness except by virtue of its affective value. So far as sensory experience goes, the rolling landscape of field and sky amid which you are disporting yourself is much the same for you, for the ploughman who is leading his team on yonder hill, for his horses, for your dog, and for those grazing sheep. Sense-organs are virtually identical in all those mammals ; but the noted sensations, the sensory bombardment, differs nevertheless hugely in you, the ploughing peasant, the dog, the horses, the sheep. From the world of sensation, that only is abstracted by each which has value in terms of active interests. Originally it is only in view of that interest, in view of a purpose useful to us, of an impulse that urges us, that the entire apparatus of sense-organs, of cognition, that seems to thrust upon us a multitude of indifferent sensations has come into being at all, and developed into its present illusory form.

When we are adopting a scientific attitude, when of set purpose we apply ourselves to investigate and describe an object, as part, say, of an imposed task, we seem concerned purely with the *quale* of the thing, our attitude is objective and realistic. But that very attitude assigns to the object of our inquiry a new value ; our abstract, disinterested, detached investigation, our strenuous effort to eliminate the ' personal equation,' to be ' objective,' is inspired by desire for accurate truth ; and the passion for truth is, after all, a passion. The *quale* of our object becomes itself an affective value, a significance in terms of our desire, our purpose, our conation.

When you are idly and helplessly lying in a bed of

convalescence, the pattern of the wall-paper, the stains of the ceiling, which you never before noticed, obtrude themselves upon you with such annoying insistence only by virtue of your shrinking from the blank of your existence, of your desire for some exercise and interest ; the rows of conventional flowers become exasperating from the penury of satisfaction which they afford to those desires that are aroused in you by returning strength.

Pure cognitive experience does not exist ; cognition is always a *cognito-affective* experience. It consists of a presented object and of the affective value of that object ; of knowledge, and of the affective significance to the organisms of that knowledge.

Every presentation *is* a feeling—though every feeling is not a presentation. In sensory perception the complex object presented, and compounded not only of the actual sensations, but also of memories and apperceptions which make up its significance, has an affective value of its own apart from that of the sensations which present it. But those sensations themselves are feelings, and, as feelings, have their own affective value. Hence many untrained thinkers, and also some trained and professed thinkers, experience some difficulty in drawing a clear distinction between the cognitive element of presentation and the affective one of pure feeling, between a pain, say, and a sensation. We commonly speak of a ' sensation of pain.' The fact is that at that primordial level the cognitive and affective elements are so intimately blended as to coalesce. A cognitive sensation, such as that which you experience when cautiously exploring the temperature of the handle of a kettle, will pass by a rapid transition into a sharp pain if you grasp the handle and find it to be too hot. A sensation is, in fact, nothing else than an affective feeling thus cautiously and tentatively put to an exploratory use ; it is a feeling adapted to cognitive and presentative purposes. And, as such, it may rise to such affective intensity that its presentational function is disregarded and obliterated in the urgency of the affective commotion. The most delicate discriminating sensation is as much a feeling as a burn, or a blow on the head ; it is only in the use that the exploratory feeling of sensation is put to that the distinction lies. To exercise its cognitive function the feeling must be so attenuated, must by the keenness of its search so forestall actual pain, that no affective value of its own shall interfere with the cognitive operation. All cognition, from sensation up to the highest functions of abstract thought, demands that detachment of disinterestedness in the feeling through which it is obtained ; its cognitive efficiency depends upon the checking of its affective value by a cognitive effort.

Primitively all affection reduces itself to the feelings of pleasantness and unpleasantness, pleasure and pain, comfort and discomfort. Pleasure and pain—*physical* pleasure and pain, of course—are the primary affections of which all other feelings whatsoever, up to our highest values, emotional, artistic, intellectual, or moral, are derivatives. Common estimation rightly recognizes the fundamental identity of two psychic states seemingly very widely different—a physical pain and a grief, the pain of a burn and that of the loss of a beloved. (A *physical* pain ! that is a very glaring contradiction ; as if a pain could be physical, a feeling material !) The physiological pain in a limb or a viscus is clearly the obstruction of its function, the interference with its activity, its partial destruction. The emotion of anguish caused by a scrap of paper that brings the news of a ' Nevermore,' is in exactly the same relation to the conations of our conceptual being as the physiological pain caused by scalding water to the conation of our dermal tissues.

The affective quality of experience shades off in intensity from the extreme throes of agony to that faint affective colouring which our surroundings cast upon us, which is perhaps hardly noticed, and which seems to approach, but never in reality reaches, a neutral state of indifference.

You may take no particular account of the impression which the room into which you are shown produces upon you, whether it is satisfying or offensive, cheerful or depressing ; but to the sensory impression which it produces there corresponds a subtle affective tone which, even more than the matter-of-fact features which you may note, constitutes their effect upon you.

Language, being a descriptive, and therefore a purely cognitive, symbolism, can never express feeling ; it can at most, like all art, suggest it. A feeling that is named is no longer a feeling, it is the presentation of a feeling, a mere cognition. When feeling is overwhelming and bursts into expression, our polished and refined instrument of articulate diction breaks down into inarticulate ejaculations, into the primitive cries and yells of the beast. Hence language is necessarily very meagre in its nomenclature of affective states, in contrast with the subtlety and elaboration of its cognitive distinctions. It has names only for affective states raised to the superlative degree —pain, anger, surprise, fear, disgust, and so forth. Our ordinary affective states are far too delicate and subtle to be distinguished by such coarse labels. It is the province of art to convey by suggestive means an affective colouring which is not to be set down in the language of scientific description.

And our thought which is bound down to the symbolism of language is thereby rendered unobservant of our own feelings, so that we remain for the most part incognizant of them unless they force themselves upon us by rising to an unusual pitch. They colour our life, our moods, and shape our activity without being taken note of by our cognitive word-consciousness ; and we marvel at the artist when he reveals to us our own unnoticed feelings.

All feeling, whether a ' physical ' feeling or an ineffable shade of emotional significance, is the effect of whatever acts upon us. Upon ' us '—that is to say, upon our own activities, our impulses and dispositions to activity. It is the modification of those dispositions, their satisfaction and stimulation, their checking and dissatisfaction, the diversified selective action of all influences—' physical ' or presentative—upon the total mass of the conative tendencies which constitute our being as a source of action. Crude physiological pain intermingled with sensation itself, if crude primary organic needs are at stake ; sublimated emotional values if it is those elaborately cultivated tastes that our culture has created, which are involved ; interests which in a larger or smaller measure arrest our attention if cognition itself is our purpose of the moment. The affective colouring of any experience is the chord which that experience strikes on the manifold tendencies of our being. As the conative tendencies involved become more abstract, more far-reaching in their glance before and after, more complex in their combinations, apperceptions and associations, affective values become correspondingly diversified and sublimated. There is much similarity between one crude physiological pain and another, between the pain of a stab, say, or that of a scald ; the exact savour and quality of an emotional value, of the feeling which a landscape, a book, a man, a political event, a situation, awakens in us, how it strikes us, faintly or forcibly, according to the directness of our interest in it, is a complex, elusive, ineffable feeling-tone, which calls for the utmost acuteness of psychological observation to seize and analyse, which it is the peculiar task of the deftest art to render and suggest. But all, from the crudest pain to violent or faint emotion and sentimental colouring of experience, are affections of our conative dispositions.

An affection, a feeling, an emotion, is, then, the experiential obverse of those conative dispositions, their mould, their form and pressure in consciousness, when they are checked or intensified ; it is the stimulation or obstruction of a conative tendency. That affective

value is the only value, is the only form in which a conative
tendency or disposition is represented in consciousness.
We do not know any conative tendency directly as such ;
that lies outside the sphere of consciousness. We only
know its imprint in feeling, in the experience of pleasure
or pain, in the variety of our affective states. And it
is in that sense that the world of affective values, of
emotions, is the *truest* world, and art the truest truth :
we deal there with the essentials and fundamentals of
our being.

Pure feeling, affective values, the breaking of an
obstructed conation into consciousness is genetically the
first aspect and element of consciousness, and is in truth
the only one of which all others are derivative. Consciousness came into the world as pain. Feeling serves to guide
the activities of life. Conditions that are favourable to
its conative impulses are represented in consciousness by
a pleasurable feeling and existing activity is stimulated ;
conditions that are unfavourable to the activity of those
impulses are represented by a feeling of discomfort, of
pain, and existing activities are inhibited. Such is the
very simple mechanism of all living reaction. It is the
whole mechanism of the behaviour of living things, of
psychic action ; all the rest is superadded elaboration.
Feeling, pure feeling of comfort or discomfort, without
any element of cognition, without any apprehension of
an objective quality in the environment, is all that is
essentially necessary—assuming any psychism to be
necessary—to the operation of the conations of life, to
the modification of reaction. And, as a matter of fact,
that is all the psychism which, if we may judge of it by
their behaviour, is to be found in the simpler forms of
life. It is all the psychic mechanism of the human infant,
which is a purely affective being. Nor is the process
essentially different in our own life and behaviour ; all
the apparatus of our cognitive powers and experience,
sensations, concepts, thoughts, exists solely in the service

of our impulses and of their conscious representation in feeling.

Cognition, as distinguished from affection or pure feeling, is not an essential, an indispensable element in the process of life ; and consequently it is not a primordial, original and innate feature of it. Cognition is a luxury. All cognitive processes, from the simplest form of sensation onwards, are an elaboration, an improvement, an acquired character which has developed out of non-cognitive forms of life and mind. They are, in fact, modified feelings.

All our psychological science has grown from the point of view of a cognitive, sensational and intellectualistic, attitude. That inveterate bias has caused all psychological problems to be approached from the starting-point of cognitive processes, of sensation with Locke and the sensationalists, of the pure intellect with Kant and the intellectualists ; while the conative activities of living beings were set aside as of secondary interest, and were left to be dealt with by Professors of Virtue.

Considered from the purely psychological standpoint, the assumption that cognition is the starting-point of psychism is false. No cognition is ' given,' no cognitive experience is thrust upon us. On the contrary, of the myriad possibilities of experience that assail our organism at every moment we sense nothing, we know nothing but what we desire to know, what it interests us to know. The mind is not a judge, comfortably seated, as it were, in its judgment-seat, before whom passes an endless procession of witnesses offering ' the testimony of the senses.' It forcibly drags by its own exertions the witnesses it requires into the limelight of consciousness.

If we consider the organism and the ambient universe from a physical point of view, there is no agency in the latter that does not in some manner affect the organism, whether it be sensed or no. It matters not whether that organism be a philosopher, an amœba, or a plant ;

it is part of the physical universe, and we are bound to assume that every ether-wave, every gravitational force, every molecular disturbance, every molar motion in that universe has, to a greater or a less degree, an inevitable physical effect upon the organism as a physical system. The revolutions of the moons of Jupiter affect the molecules of my brain. Unless we set aside every physical conception, every change and agency in the physical world must needs have its repercussion in the organism. Of all those physical effects on the organism what is represented in sensation is but an infinitesimally small fraction. Our sensations, our cognitions, far from being a representation, a reflection as in a mirror, of the external universe, are but an absurdly minute fragment of the impressions which the external universe, all unknown to us, actually makes upon our physiological beings. There are more things in heaven and earth than are dreamed of in our sensory cognition. We human beings, with our highly elaborated sense-organs, our cunningly contrived eyes and ears, and exploring hands, can actually sense but a few miserable odd shreds of the physical influences which incessantly ply our bodily structure. We are no more omnisensing than we are omniscient. Cathodic rays pass through and through our bodies, producing the most profound physiological action, yet leave us sensorily incognizant ; we stand by the side of a wireless telegraphic apparatus which Herzian waves cause to sizzle furiously, and we sense nothing ; we stand in the field of force of a magnet that will stop our watch, and which does not produce in us the slightest sensation. The range of our sensation is as that of the visible spectrum compared to the whole length of the solar spectrum—a mere fraction. Indeed, our sensory faculties are in many respects considerably more reduced than those of the lower animals. Our olfactory sense is degenerate and vestigial compared to that of the dog ; our civilized vision is far less keen than that of a savage or of a bird. Ants and bees react

5

to waves of the spectrum which are quite unperceived by us. The amœba itself is sensitive to chemical changes which to us are undiscernible ; myxomycetes respond to gaseous emanations which we are unable to detect.

To suppose that all those unsensed physical actions, and thousands more of which we have no inkling, impinge on every molecule of our organism without producing any effect at all upon the psychic aspect of that organism, is quite impossible except on the most extreme dualistic view of mental isolation. Unquestionably every one of those physical impressions has its effect, deep and momentous, upon our psychic activities. But that effect is not sensory, is not cognitive. The actions of things upon us is, as we said, represented by feeling, not by presentative feeling necessarily, not by sensation. And we know that many unsensed physical states of our environment, atmospheric conditions and pressures, electrical disturbances, do affect us in our moods, in the general tone of our vitality and activity. It is hardly to be doubted that the whole physical universe thus enters causally into the determination of our activity, of our behaviour, of our reactions, of our feelings ; that uncognized influence of the whole physical universe is one set of factors, wholly obscure to us, in our mental causation. But so far as sensory cognition is concerned it is only represented by a quite insignificant little bundle of sensations.

Our sensory experience, then, is not by a long way coextensive with the impression of the external world upon our organism. It is not a mechanical reflection, as in a mirror, of those impressions. It is but a very small selection of those impressions, which are the same for the lowest as for the highest organism. The impression of an external agency and a sensation are two widely different things ; and sensory experience is not something impressed by the external world on our organs, something ' given,' but it is something picked out, seized, selected by the organism out of the mass of impressions impinging upon it.

If we trace the evolution of cognition backwards, divesting it one by one of those elaborations which it has assumed in the course of development, we shall first witness the vanishing of general ideas, of conceptual thought, of all re-presentation whatsoever. Cognition will be reduced to direct sense-cognition. Sensation will further simplify itself ; our organism no longer has eyes, ears, olfactory organs, or tactile corpuscles. The differentiation and discrimination of sensory impressions become gradually less and less ; various amplitudes of ether waves are no longer distinguished, nor the impact of molecules from that of larger bodies. Ultimately the issue of such a process of backward de-differentiation would logically appear to be to reduce all the diversity of our sensory experience to one vague wholly undifferentiated sensory continuum, a sort of blended smell-taste-sight-touch sensation. That apparently logical conclusion is, however, wholly erroneous ; and it is only owing to the failure of psychologists to grasp the nature of sensory cognition that they are led to such an antinomy as the notion of an 'undifferentiated sensation,' a flatly self-contradictory conception, for sensation in its essence and origin *is* a differentiation.

The backward limit of simplification of sensation is not an 'undifferentiated sensory continuum,' but no sensation at all. Sensation does not become undifferentiated, but passes into a purely affective state in which no element of cognition enters. The primitive organism does not sense solidity, form, heat ; it feels satisfactions and dissatisfactions, it cognizes nothing. As we descend the psychological scale we do not come upon undifferentiated sensation, but the cognitive element rapidly dwindles, the affective element bulks more and more as the chief, and ultimately the sole, constituent of experience. In animals there is very little left of that contemplative, knowledge-acquiring attitude ascribed to the soul. Curiosity has a very utilitarian function; cognition only exists as the symptom, the sign of a vital affection; sensation is but the clue to food, to safety, to reproductive activity, the warning signal of danger. Present a diamond scarf-pin to a new-born human infant. No effort of yours will succeed in attracting his attention; the diamond has no value for it, its rolling eyes do not see it, its ears are deaf to your blandishments. But stick the pin into it; you will at once elicit vivid manifestations of experience—experience which is not at all cognitive, but purely affective. The new-born human infant, like the lower forms of life, is a purely affective psychological mechanism.

Sensory power, more generally all cognitive power, is not something ' given,' a primary datum of organic existence; it is a product, a result of evolution. Sensation, no less than imagination or conceptual thought, has been brought into being in the course of organic evolution. It has evolved, like every other manifestation of life, because it was useful—useful, that is, to the operation of the conative tendencies of organic life. Cognition has developed out of feeling; nay, more, feeling itself out of no feeling.

If feeling can only take place as the concomitant of change in the vital activities of an organism brought about by changes in the conditions of those activities, it follows that an organism the vital needs of which were continuously and uniformly satisfied would be devoid of feeling; just as our physiological function of respiration is, so long as normally carried out without check, un-accompanied by feeling. Such an organism is not an imaginary one, here hypothetically conceived. It is, on the contrary, a familiar and common form of living organization; but in order to find it we must go back beyond the amœba even, beyond the beginnings of animal life. The protozoon is by no means the most primitive type of living organism. Far from it. It, on the contrary, represents a very definite stage, a turning-point, a revolutionary climacteric in the course of organic evolution. It is an animal. Animals are predatory forms of life ; they live on prey, they are incapable of existing except by preying : no animal life can exist without vegetable life. Animals live, ultimately, on vegetables ; they subsist on the nitrogenous products which vegetables, by means of chlorophyll, form out of atmospheric carbon by utilizing the energy of sunlight. Animals, like all parasitic forms, have lost a power which they no longer need, having adopted the much more convenient plan of leaving plants to perform the work, and eating them. There still exist some transition forms which do both the carbon extraction by means of chlorophyll and the preying and eating. The appearance of animals was the establishment of a predatory aristocracy which exploited a defenceless class and lived on the fruits of their labour.

In vegetable life, then, conative impulses—here mainly concerned with assimilating the chemical material needful to the metabolism of vital existence—do not take the form of a questing effort intermittingly achieving its end, but of a continuous appetence continuously satisfied. The plant bathes in its food, it does not search for it and procure it. The object of satisfaction is always there, the conative process is purely assimilative. And accordingly all the processes of cognitive exploration are superfluous, and are absent. Even feeling is, doubtless, rudimentary, dim, and crepuscular, if it be present ; plants behave when subjected to violence like inorganic objects. It is needless to stop to discuss here whether in such intermittences as do occur in the conditions of vegetable life, resulting in slow, sluggish ' tropisms ' towards light or support, whether in some reproductive processes and, exceptionally, in the peculiar reactions of carnivorous plants, we have the indications of some rudimentary form of affective experience. Personally I do not doubt that it is so. But it suffices us to note that in the vegetable world, where in general no search for the means of satisfaction takes place, no sharp reaction to unfavourable circumstances is observable, and no development and differentiation of sensory organs or of nervous apparatus, which plays so conspicuous a part in animal evolution, no evolution of cognitive means, has taken place.

Those developments and devices are the appanage of questing, preying, hunting forms of life. They are not primary attributes of life, but are as much as the most subtle elaboration of structure or of function, an achievement, a product of conative forces. It is out of a purely affective form of experience that sensation has been developed and differentiated.

Our primitive animalcule has derived much enhanced satisfaction and efficiency from the assimilation of the ready-made proteid substances of vegetable organisms. Its metabolic conations, instead of slowly manufacturing protoplasm from the ambient fluid, have found a much easier and more effectual channel of satisfaction in the assimilation of other organisms. The intermittent event of contact with these sets up henceforth activities directed to their assimilation. On contact with a diatom, gases, exhalations, issue thence which molecularly affect protozoan organization. But these are not, in the origin of life, scented, tasted, sensed ; they are merely pleasant ; they constitute a purely affective stimulus which sets assimilative processes to work.

But let us suppose that our primitive, predatory animalcule, its appetite now thoroughly alive and keen, meets with the following adventure. The usual feelings symptomatic of an approaching meal are present, our voraciousness is on the tiptoe of expectation, our organism reacts to the usual stimulus. But . this time something appears to go wrong, our assimilative efforts are thwarted, our digestive impulse is not satisfied. On the contrary, instead of a state of satisfaction, the result is a decided discomfort, a pain. Reaction to the customary stimulus has resulted in dissatisfaction instead of satisfaction. The fact is that instead of a succulent diatom we have swallowed a flint. The result of such a lamentable experience is to damp the impulsiveness of our voracity, to inhibit our deglutitional reflex, as the physiologist would put it. The conative impulse is not abolished ; it is too fundamental for that ; but it is modified. It becomes hesitant. The affective feeling is no longer a reliable stimulus. The organism still reacts to the pleasant sense of apprehending a meal, but more cautiously. Is that pleasant feeling the genuine thing or are we going to be cruelly deceived ? The question is not, of course, asked by the primitive animalcule, but nevertheless—to make an age-long story short—a new conative impulse becomes gradually set up. Its object is to note more precisely the nature of that feeling, to discriminate between the promising and the unpromising feeling, to pick out from the affective continuum the differentiating signs It aims, in short, at cognition : the experience from being purely affective assumes a cognitive aspect. The organism learns to distinguish from an originally un-differentiated affective continuum the cognitive marks which promise satisfaction from those which threaten dissatisfaction. And thus in time cognition proper emerges out of the affective state, sensation is brought into being out of the affective result of unrealized conation.

You will, of course, interject that the above account of the adventure of our predatory animalcule is highly imaginative. But here again there is enough of rudi-mentary protozoic psychology left in all the descendants of the protozoon, ourselves included, to check the hypothesis. The process which I have described is no more than may be observed any day in the most highly developed organism, making due allowance for the fact

that the latter happens to be in possession of an already
formed and highly differentiated and specialized cognitive
apparatus. That apparatus does not, as a matter of fact,
perform its functions at all except at the call of affective
needs. Exactly similar to the process above described
in our primitive protozoon are those illustrated by the
new-born chick in the classical observations of Professor
Lloyd-Morgan.[1]

" With regard to the objects which the domestic chicks peck,
one may say that they strike at first with perfect impartiality
at *anything* of suitable size . . . anything and everything, not too
large, that can or cannot be seized is pecked at, and, if possible,
tested in the bill. . . . There does not seem to be any congenital
discrimination. . . . This is a matter of individual acquisition. . . .
A young chick two days old, for example, had learned to pick out
pieces of yolk from others of white of egg. . . . I cut little bits
of orange peel of about the same size as the pieces of yolk, and one
of them was soon seized, but at once relinquished, the chick shaking
his head. Seizing another, he held it for a moment in his bill, but
then dropped it and scratched the base of his beak. That was
enough ; he could not again be induced to seize a piece of orange
peel. The obnoxious material was now removed and pieces of
yolk of egg substituted, but they were left untouched, being probably
taken for orange peel. Subsequently he looked at the yolk with
hesitation, but presently pecked doubtfully, not seizing, but merely
touching. Then he pecked again, seized and swallowed."

If you consider even the psychology of the chick to
be too far removed from your own, observe the human
baby. He possesses the self-same organs of cognition as
yourself, but they pour no world of sensation into his
experient soul. He has eyes and does not see, ears and
he does not hear. He has a voracious appetite and,
like the amœba, like the chick, will suck in anything
into the pseudopods of his lips—a finger, a pencil, a tin
soldier, a rose, a model aeroplane. One of the chief
functions of his nurse is to extract unsuitable foreign
bodies from his slavering little mouth. Only repeated
experience of satisfaction and dissatisfaction will gradually
lead him to differentiate by means of sensory impressions

[1] *Habit and Instinct*, pp. 40–42.

between comestible and incomestible articles. Only affective values will guide his way to sensory cognition. Even a fully developed inherited sensory apparatus can only come into operation through education by affective feelings. And in ourselves no cognition can take place unless introduced into consciousness by affective values.

Sensory organs are only developed where they can, in ordinary circumstances, serve the utilities of conative interests manifested in feeling. Power of tactile sensation is distributed on the outer surface of the body, and proportionally to the uses to which it can be put, but it is absent from internal organs ; the brain itself can be hacked about with a scalpel without the slightest sensation being produced. Undifferentiated experience is still with us purely affective, contains no cognitive element whatsoever. We are in health unconscious of our health, unconscious of the operation of a thousand conative impulses. We breathe and assimilate, and nothing referring to those processes is represented in consciousness. But let the function be disturbed, let the conative tendency be obstructed, let the supply of air fail, and at once we have a pressing experience thrust upon us, an experience in which there is no element of cognition, but only feeling, the feeling of discomfort, the general quality of pain. Only those feelings which in the course of evolution have assumed a useful, warning, exploring function have undergone cognitive differentiation. The rest have remained affective, cœnæsthetic. And as we ourselves are born purely affective beings, as in more primitive forms of humanity the affective character of experience obtains to the exclusion of the cognitive, so as we recede in the scale of organic evolution all cognition rapidly dwindles, and the experience of the organism remains purely or largely affective.

It is inevitable that all that multitude of influences which the universe exercises upon our organisms, and of which only an infinitesimal portion is represented in sensation, should in reality affect us, should go to make up our affective state at any moment. That affective state is only in a limited measure produced by what we perceive ; it is mainly produced by what we do not perceive, by influences that are not cognized. What we cognize as sensation consists of elements extracted from that affective continuum, because we need them as signs. They are extracted, analysed out, perceived, by being attended to, by a cognitive effort urged by appetite or fear, which desires to feel more keenly, more vividly, to make feeling more delicate and acute so as to anticipate actual painful feeling, to pick up the track of desired objects. Sensation is constantly thus *educated*, rendered more acute by actual effort, by use, as with workers in colours, musicians, tasters, perfumers. Everyone knows the old experiment suggested by Hack Tuke of concentrating one's attention upon a given point of our body, our little finger, say, for ten minutes or so. (The ease with which the experiment is performed differs considerably in various people.) Sensations will make their appearance in your little finger, tinglings, muscular sensations, twitchings, sometimes acute and vivid sensations. Those sensations cannot be supposed to be created ; beyond doubt they are present as part of our general affective tone all the time, but they are elicited as sensations by attending to them.

Our intellectualistic psychology declares, as might be expected, that affections are the *result* of sensations, that sensations *produce* feelings and emotions. It is quite true, of course, that when once sensation or any form of cognition has been developed for the express purpose of signifying, of serving as a sign, the symbol of an affective value, that sign calls up the affective state which it is its function to announce and anticipate. And thus the sequence comes to be reversed : the sensation gives rise to the affection instead of the affection leading to the sensation. All art, literature, music, employ sensation, sensational symbols, in order to evoke affective states, emotional moods. Your musician will undertake to set up in you a flutter of the most disembodied affective moods, of exultation or tenderness, melancholy or joy, by propagating from the vibrations of a catgut waves that shall strike upon your tympanum. Sensation produces affection. But the order in which the process of artistic production originates is exactly the reverse. The affective mood of the artist evokes sensory symbols and images, and he uses these, sounds, colours, forms, to translate, to express, his purely affective mood, making them *significant*. Sensations give rise to affective conditions because they have become symbolic of them; but they can only do so, acquire that symbolic value, precisely owing to the fact that they were originally an integral part of those affective values; they are efficient symbols of affections by virtue of their origin out of them.

For that differentiation of affection into cognition to take place it is necessary not only that experience should be diversified in time, but that it should also be differentiated in space. So long as the obstructed conation is uniformly diffused over the entire organism it remains pure feeling. An enormous pressure of thirty-two pounds weighs upon every inch of our bodies; we are entirely incognizant of it. Let that pressure be released, as in the ascent of a mountain or in flight, the disturbance becomes indeed represented in consciousness, but not as the sensation of an external event; we feel unwell, we have a general sense of malaise, we have no sense of lessened pressure. The temperature of our ambient is uniformly raised or lowered; *we* feel hot or cold, we feel, that is, not that the circumambient air is hot or cold, but that we ourselves are hot or cold. The feeling is entirely subjective, it is not projected into any external object. Frogs have been roasted alive by gradually raising the temperature of the metal plate on which they were placed, without their moving a muscle to escape ; the feeling was not referable to any external event. The relation of externality, the relation between subject and object, does not exist so long as the impression affects the entire organism ; nor does it exist for the organism whose whole supplies are derived from the fluids and gases in which it bathes. In order that the external world and spacial relations should come into existence, it is necessary that there should be a differential feeling between one part of the organism and another, a differential activity of those parts, a directional reaction.

With us sense-cognition has come to be essentially massive, bound, that is, with the idea of molar movements ; we think in terms of matter, of solids. Movement means to us the wide sweep of the limb, the play of skeletal muscles by which our body is transported through space, or the wholesale locomotion of huge masses of matter, the falling or projected stone, the astral motion of a globe. And objects are solids with a widely extended surface which we can mentally sweep over with our hand. The logical analysis of our sensations by introspective, genetically oblivious psychology, leads us down to a sensory experience of touch, of the resistance offered by a solid body to the pressure exercised by our fingers. That, we say, is the typical and fundamental sensation into which all others logically resolve themselves. Sight is only a sort of shorthand which represents to us what sensations of touch a closer contact would yield. Distance similarly represents the amount of muscular effort interposed between us and the exercise of pressure on an object. Sounds, smells, tastes, are likewise aerial or molecular impacts : and they do not, moreover, except by association, yield any presentation of external existence. Only the massive sensations of pressure can do that, and are therefore the fundamental sensory experiences *par excellence* to which all others are reducible.

So far analytic intellectualistic psychology, based on the differentiated modes of cognition of our organism alone. But physiologically traced down, those massive solid, molar conceptions reduce themselves to much more minute dimensions, resolve themselves into molecular, chemical sensations like those of smell and taste. And if our interpretation is correct, it is those molecular, chemical sensations vestigially represented in us by the senses of smell, taste, temperature, and not the massive sensations of touch, which are the original, the oldest, the primary sensations, and it is out of them that our ' higher senses ' have grown. They are, as it were, inter- mediate phases between exteriorly projected sensation and pure feeling, between cognitive and affective experience. In themselves they do not contain any element of exte- riority, scarcely of localization ; we could not from them derive any concept of an external world. In fact, they still closely approach to purely subjective sensations, to pure feeling ; and are but vaguely differentiated according to sensory values. Our nomenclature of smells and tastes, like our nomenclature of feelings, is indefinite and rudimentary, and still refers in the main to affective values ; the rough, unsophisticated classification of those sensations is into ' nice ' and ' nasty.'

And it is noteworthy in this connection that sensations of smell, although they have in us become quite rudimentary and cognitively unimportant, are still of all our sensations those which have in the highest degree the power of reviving affective states. Nothing will bring back to us so vividly the actual affective atmosphere of a past situation, of a person, of a place, as a scent, the vague, undefinable olfactory impression. The associative link with our affective states, with the real significance to us in emotional terms of the past, is closest with the chemical sense of smell.

It is those intimate chemical forms of sensation, then, which probably were genetically original, the first differentiation out of affective feeling ; and while they were the only ones they left the external world as yet unborn.

The molar plane of sensory cognition implies the molar, directed movement of a motile, questing organism ; that movement which is to us the type of action, of behaviour. It implies an organic differentiation : no longer does the organism react homogeneously as a whole, but the reaction of the whole expresses itself as a co-ordinated and differentiated action of its *parts*. But this molar action, the characteristic of the preying food-quest, is, no less than the most rudimentary sensory process, a molecular change. Our power of movement which calls to mind the power to raise our arm aloft in response to a nervous impulse transmitted from the brain, is really (still speaking physiologically) the power to effect very minute changes in certain portions of the colloid substances of our striped muscles. We do not move masses, we move molecules. The levering up of a boulder is a chemical operation.

And chemical sensations are not presentations of extended objects, are not spacially extended.

The transition from that diffuse unspacial feeling and acting is, like that from pure feeling to sensation of any kind, definitely traceable to the animal food-quest. The end of the preying animal is no longer to assimilate a quantum of energy, but to enclose an *object* as the *means* to that assimilation of energy. The searching organism came to react not to the emanations alone of its prey, but to its contact. It felt it as something resistant to be englobed. In the amœboid organism englobing and seizing its prey was the first origin of that relation which was to become the refrain of German metaphysics, the pendulum swing of ' subject ' and ' object.' The prey, henceforth the object of desire, was felt, encircled, devoured. It was the first *not-me*, not an object of rarefied academic-philosophic contemplation, but of crude, voracious animal appetite, the prototype of all *not-me's*, of the external universe of contemplative thought.

An object, a material thing, is still for us essentially something seizable, something that we can mentally encompass and embrace, something which is extended, as we say, which has form. It is a curious relic of that origin that our thought is almost incapable of imaging the obverse of compassable form, to picture an object *from the inside.* Try to form a mental picture of the inside of a sphere, of a polyhedron, of your clothes inwardly viewed ; scarcely can you succeed in doing that ; the mind slips involuntarily into the external view of the object ; it requires to prehend form in order to apprehend it at all. It still seizes the object of its cognition as a prey.

Not only is that perception of extended solid matter the presentation of the molar activity of seizing it, it is, in its original and direct form, the action itself. To ' feel,' to palpate, is but a slightly attenuated and hesitatingly exploratory form of seizing, grasping, engulfing. The operation of sensing matter is carried out by the act itself of manipulating it.

With the alertness of life to avail itself of every opportunity, another quite different form of sensation, the perception of luminous waves of various lengths, has become utilized to forestall the actual palpatory act, by associating with it the visual form of sensation. Apart from that association the effect of light is a purely chemical one—one of the first and most important forms of chemical energy, indeed, utilized by organic life in its metabolic reactions—and it has no quality whatever of spaciality, of extension, of materiality about it. That association is purely a matter of empirical education, of individual education even. To patients operated on for congenital cataract there is no suggestion of form or extended space in visual impressions ; as in the famous case of Cheselden's patient who described all objects as " touching his eyes."

In certain strange cerebral disorders, known as ' apraxia,'
or ' psychic blindness,' the structural channels of association between the visual and motor centres are affected ;
the patient's vision is quite unimpaired, he sees perfectly,
but things have no longer any *meaning*, they are un-
recognizable, they are no longer material objects. His
motor powers are as intact as his sight, but they can no
longer be used in association with it. It is through the
circuitous device of that association that a form of sensory
feeling which is in itself wholly destitute of spacial
qualities, which presents nothing but an unextended and
unexternal modification of feeling, has come, through
its far-flung synthesis and symbolic representation of
molar movement, to be the ' dominant sense ' of conceptual consciousness ; causing the ' material world ' to
be ' imaged ' in the mind's vision. The mind will thence-
forth contemplate ' images,' think in terms of spacially
extended solid ' objects.'

By that presentation of molar motion all other sensory
forms of presentation have come to be superseded, and
dismissed as ' secondary attributes of matter.' That
evaluation is the consequence of the fact that the molar
motion which matter represents has itself superseded the
mere chemical, diffuse, intimate reactions, which constituted the primary activities of life, and which have
now become degraded to the level of ' physiological,'
' vegetative ' acts, a secondary dualism being thus set up
between ' life ' and ' mind.'

But the original presentation and the fundamental one
was, for all that, a diffuse, unextended, unexternalized
modification of feeling ; and the original and fundamental
reactions and activities of life were formless, chemical,
molecular, unextended. The molar acts which seize,
grasp, and move—and which are reducible in physiological
analysis to chemical, molecular reactions—and the material
objects of those acts, pertain to the order of instrumentality, of *means*. And in fact, for all the illusions of our

materialistic conceptual thought, matter can never be a real *object*, an object of our conation. Nobody desires a material object as such, nobody has a wish to possess matter. The material object which we desire, the material behaviour by which we effect changes in matter and seek to compass it, are never ends in themselves, but always— as for the first preying amœba—means to reactions which have nothing spacial about them, to assimilations that are not molar, to feelings which have no extended form.

CHAPTER IV

DEVELOPMENT OF COGNITION

EPISTEMOLOGICAL psychology has elaborated and refined its distinctions between the various forms and grades of cognition. Chasms of discriminating differentiation have been set between the various cognitive processes of sensation, perception, conception, ideation, intellect, thought, which have come to appear fundamental ; discriminations which an ingenious analysis may carry much farther, as in those subtle Kantian distinctions between ' the reason ' and ' the understanding '—' *Vernunft* ' and ' *Verstand.*' In spite of modern developments, the old notion of separate ' faculties ' appears to linger yet, insidiously disguised, in the realm of cognitive psychology ; and the ' faculty ' which senses an ' intuition ' is generally regarded as having little in common with the abstract thought of the philosopher that classifies the categories of the intellect. It is not, indeed, so very long ago since the power of conceptual thought was regarded as a special ' human faculty ' obviously and utterly distinct in nature from the crude instincts and sensations of animals.

Genetically viewed and analysed, the facts testify to the exact opposite of such a view. There are no separate ' faculties ' ; there is an operation of *cognition*, and the essential mode of that operation is the same from the dimmest rudiments of sensation to the highest flights of discursive and abstract thought. Sensory perceptions are not *data* of experience, the bricks, as it were, out of which have been built up the high structures of conceptual thought. In the cognitive activity of sensory perception, even in its most rudimentary form, are implicated in all essential respects the modes of operation of every cognitive process up to their highest phases of development. Cognitive processes, from those which modify the reaction of an animalcule to those which constitute the thought of the philosopher, differ in degree of elaboration only ; in the essential principles of their activity they are fundamentally identical.

Every cognitive process, whether it be the most primitive form of nascent sensation or the most abstract analysis of metaphysical thought, is an act of *comparison*. In the one as in the other there is this judgment, ' This is like (or unlike) that.' Primitive sensation differentiates out of the affective continuum the cognitive elements of likeness or unlikeness which serve to forestall the affective value of experience—to recognize or distinguish that which leads to pain and that which leads to satisfaction. It is an act of comparison between two affective states, which recognizes their likeness or unlikeness. You will find in Kant nothing beyond a series of such comparisons. Every predicate that we assign to an object is the term of a comparison of that object with another object or class of objects.

When a primitive protozoon impelled by the conative needs of its life gropes towards their satisfaction and lights instead upon a dissatisfaction, retracting itself from the stimulus which it at first sought, a contrast is set up between the situation to which the dispositions of the organism were attuned and that which comes upon them. The actual situation is organically contrasted with the one which the organic forces were prepared to meet. The latter term of the relation is the reproduction of the previous habitual reaction so far as the organism is concerned, a representation, a memory, howsoever rudimentarily constituted by the renewal of the conative attitude called for by the apparent repetition of a former situation.

Higher, much higher, in the scale of evolution some affectively prominent cognition, sign, or sensation, or a small group of such, serves as a symbol for the whole group of experiences : the scent of the quarry is followed, the roar of the enemy is feared. Here the actual experience, the seizing of the quarry, the mawling by the enemy, is not awaited ; it is forestalled, replaced by a sensory sign which has come to be indicative, symbolic of it. The present term of the comparison, the experience, is symbolic, and the symbol, by its function, identifies it with a past experience. Every sensory act is a protention in time of the actual moment ; it looks before and after. It reproduces a previous affective attitude, and anticipates an impendent experience ; it is a means to the modification of the latter.

The comparing activity is the same whether it is applied to the exploration of the environment or, as ingenuity, or practical reason, to the discovery of means. The means employed by animal or human ingenuity to deal with a novel situation are drawn from activities previously employed for another purpose. Their discovery and application is a comparison of the present situation with those in which the means have proved efficient. When, for example, the path of traffic of foraging ants is blocked by an unsurmountable obstacle, the activities habitually employed by the insects in constructing their storehouses suggests itself as a means of dealing with the present problem, and the ants set to digging a tunnel under the obstacle.

Always a past experience or conative effort is compared with the present. It is not until the highest steps of mental evolution have been approached that memory, symbolic representation of past situations, grows gradually to be more or less independent of the actual present situation, and is evoked by the mere play of conative impulses. Thought in terms of symbols having an affective value independently of the actual presentation of the symbol (sensation), representation without the assistance of instant experience, has then become possible.

The great achievement which created the ' human faculty ' and dug between man and every other living organism that yawning abyss which came to be the Cartesian gulf between soul and mechanism, between man and brute, was solely the elaborate development of a perfected symbolism—the word. It is the invention of that symbolism out of the emotional cry, the call, the warning signal, the omatopoietic sound, which has brought about the possibility of human thought. The fixed symbol has rendered possible the evolution of abstraction, has forced its development in a geometrical progression which has transformed cognition from the amœba's sensation into the discursive reason of the philosopher. But in that prodigious transformation nothing in the essential process has been changed. Sensations, no less than words, are symbolic presentations of differences and similarities, which relate past, present, and future experience.

In the growth of language the first descriptive words (cognitive in function, as distinguished from the affective cries, chants, exclamations of emotion) are not verbs, are not nouns, but adjectives, that is, predicates. The subject of the primitive sentence is pointed to with the finger, the other term of the comparison, the predicate, is alone expressed. The noun, the name, the verb, are derivatives of the adjective. Thus in Sanscrit *deva*, shining, comes to signify the god ; *surya*, splendid, comes to signify the sun ; *akva*, rapid, becomes the name of the horse. The intellect seizes upon the striking, the distinctive quality of the object, and predicates it of it.

The act of predication which is the form of all thought, of all judgment, is a comparison, a differentiation of the present object from a represented object, or its subsumption under the likeness of another. When I say, ' That apple is red,' I am comparing it with other apples, with other objects that are not red. Were the whole world incardinate, no predication, no comparison, and no sensation of colour would be possible. It is in the increasing nicety of distinguishing analysis, and in the broadening abstractness of generalizing assimilation that the triumphs of human thought are manifested.

It was one of the debates of eighteenth-century thought whether the particular or the general was the starting-point of cogitation. The question rested upon a confusion. All cognition, all thought, develops primitively in view, and by virtue of its immediate utilitarian functions alone. No distinction is ever drawn unless it is forced upon the organism by a vital and urgent interest. Hence experiences and objects which are identical in their values in terms of the interests at stake are not distinguished. To the primitive organism all things good to eat are cognitively identical. To the new-born mammal all that can be sucked is of equal value and remains undistinguished ; the unsatisfactory experience of cheated appetite alone leads the lamb, the human baby, to differentiate between a tuft of wool, a finger, and the nipple. Baby, again, learns to recognize, that is, to assimilate to antecedent experience, the somewhat terrifying object ' dada,' and only later to distinguish between various ' dadas.' It makes the acquaintance of the object ' geegee,' and comes to distinguish it from the object ' moocow ' with which at first it confounded it. That primitive confusion is not at all an assimilation, a subsumption, but a failure to distinguish. Assimilation proper is the part of higher thought which *re*-unites under perceived likenesses what primitive thought has distinguished and separated. There are thus in the progress of all cognition three stages : (1) primitive confusion, (2) discrimination and distinction, and (3) the perception of the fundamental likeness under the distinction. It is true, then, as Leibniz contended against Locke and his school, that the evolution of conceptual thought proceeds from the general to the particular ; but the primitive ' general ' is not a cognitive achievement, it is, on the contrary, a failure to distinguish. And there is all the difference in the world between the thought which is too confused to distinguish, and that which subsumes and assimilates. The vice of thought of the dogmatic blockhead against whom one argues in vain is, on the other hand, mainly a failure to assimilate ; as if, having perceived the distinction between one ' dada ' and another, one should fail to recognize the similarity between all men.

When cognition for its own sake, to know, to understand, has itself, in higher human thought, become a desire, a goal of conation, likeness is sought under diversity ; the ground likeness is the fundamental, the essential, the diversity is the superficial, the contingent. And the thought of the thinker probes the universe of experience in quest of the ultimate, fundamental likeness of all being, and travels on its path towards the subsumption of all happenings under the law of their action, of the Many under the One.

That portentous evolution from sensation upwards has depended upon the perfecting of the symbolism by which one or both terms of the comparison are represented, and the wonders of the ' human faculty ' are the result of the possibilities opened up by the symbolic system of language ; to that power of the sign rather than to any very peculiar power of more elaborate comparison or of representation, of memory.

Representative memory has come to be regarded as the most striking and characteristic power of higher consciousness. It is one which fills us with wonder when we consider it, one which we tend to regard, in our marvel at its performances, as well-nigh the essence of mind. That I should be able to evoke out of nothing, as it were, a picture, an object of contemplation, which does not exist in the actual world before me ; that this picture, this abstract idea, which I gaze at with my ' mind's eye ' should be the real content of my consciousness, the object of my attention, to the exclusion of the actual world that impinges upon me—it is little wonder that I should regard that power as the supreme privilege of mind, the marvel of it which sets it apart from the unsentient universe moored and bound to the actual. It is that power to have something in my mind which is not in the world before me, which, more than anything else, suggests the conception of mind as something independently existing, a separate ' substance,' other than the gross, actual, material world.

In speculating upon the *modus operandi* of that power the first vague explanation that suggests itself is that, in some manner, previous sensory experiences are ' stored ' in the mind ; that there exist in the mind certain archives in which records of sensory experiences are filed for future reference, as a series of little photographs, say, of which an enormous number are pigeon-holed in the brain, to be brought out and inspected when required.

That ingenuous conception can no longer be seriously countenanced. There are no little photographs. What primarily tends to be reproduced is, of course, the reaction itself of the organism to a given situation. That is the distinctive property of a living system of energy—to be able to repeat its reactions. In the absence of the situation, the reaction is not repeated, but the disposition to such a repetition is nevertheless there, and what in consciousness corresponds to that disposition is not a sensation, but a pure feeling, an affective state.

It is extraordinary that introspective psychology should ever have imagined that the memory of a sensation resembles a sensation, that the memory of yesterday's dinner resembles any sensation of the dinner, or that the memory of a blow on the head resembles a blow on the head. No one has ever been able to perform such a feat as to ' reproduce a sensation.' We do not pick out photographs from the pigeon-holes of our archives, we assume the affective attitude corresponding to a past experience, an attitude with which not a glimmer of sensation is connected. Memory does not in idle moments turn over the leaves of a sensory record, but rehearses the affective values, the emotional colouring with which it has at one time or another vibrated. It is that affective tone which in turn sets quivering the sensory state which may reproduce the cognition abstracted from the sensual experience (not the sensory experience itself). The picture, the photograph, is not the cause of the mnemonic experience, but, in a very imperfect form, the possible result of the affective reproduction, a result which may quite well be, and very generally is, entirely absent.

I was reading in bed the other night a very dry and technical book of philosophy, my attention being appropriately concentrated on the abstract argument, when suddenly, in the middle of a sentence, I became vividly conscious of an undefined feeling, a feeling of a previous experience, of a situation in which I had previously found myself, a feeling with which no sensory image whatever, no definite sensation, was connected, only describable as a sense of exhilaration and well-being, of breathing freely, of gladness and health and joy of life ; and I knew that somewhere, at some time, just that same chord of feeling had been struck in me. The feeling, for all its disembodiedness and vagueness, was so vivid in tone that I was greatly interested in the phenomenon, and set about ' psycho-analysing ' to endeavour to elucidate it. I was fortunate enough to succeed. It was a clear summer night, and not many miles from the lower Thames. Presently I heard the clear, though distant sound of the siren of a small steamer. At once the sound harmonized completely with the tone of the feeling I had experienced ; and then the images associated with that feeling at once made their appearance. I was leaning over the smooth, age-worn, yellow marble of a balcony looking out on the Grand Canal in Venice, with the Dogana and Giudecca before me, and there reached me with the peculiar tone of sound over still water, the call of the siren of one of the small Lido steamers from the Riva degli Schiavoni.

As in like experiences which everyone will be able to recall, the tone of feeling is reproduced quite independently of sensory images which may or may not be present. We exaggerate altogether the power and accuracy of sensual memories. When the affective state corresponding to those sensations is revived, the illusion is produced that the sensations themselves are revived. No sensation is ever revived. And the whole sensory representation is an illusion arising from the *projection* of the sensory experience through the affective tone. We imagine that we could reproduce quite clearly the sight of a familiar street, the appearance of an absent friend. Put that belief to the test. You will be altogether at a loss to describe accurately either the sky-line of the street which is most tritely familiar to you, or the features of your friend, the exact shape of his nose, say, unless you happen to have specially *noted* it. What we remember is a 'general impression,' a local colour, the manner and mannerisms, the tone of voice of our friends. 'Unless you have specially noted it '—in that qualification lies the real key to sensory memory. A building, say, which you have merely looked at with the idle curiosity of a tourist, will be 'remembered' by you merely in an affective way as a 'general impression,' and if asked to sketch it or to describe some particulars about it, how many windows it has, for instance, the illusoriness of your memory image will be at once exposed. You may, however, have studied it more closely, you may have noted this or that particular feature of it accurately, cognitively; in that case you will remember that it has three doors, say, with full rounded arches, eight pointed windows, and so forth. But observe the character of that mental noting ; it extracts elements in a purely cognitive manner, and they are remembered in the same way, that is, in an intellectual way, as a statement for the most part that could be put into words, rather than as an image. The image is not remembered, but *reconstructed* from the statement. Only a mere schematic image can be thus committed to memory, not at all a visual impression. You are perfectly familiar with the appearance of your absent friend and totally unable to say whether his nose is straight or curved at the bridge, unless you have noted the fact. Your artist friend will sketch you from memory a striking likeness of So-and-so ; but his ability to do so depends upon the fact that he has made a particular note, an analysis from the cognitive point of view of his characteristic features ; he has committed them to memory with an artist's observation. We note nothing cognitively unless urged by a special interest to do so. We are satisfied with the ' general impression ' which suffices quite well for all our purposes, and our representation, our memory, cannot be fuller than our presentation. It is, on the contrary, by many degrees more vague and indefinite. A good memory in regard to some particular class of objects of cognition is merely the more interested cognitive noting of the presentation. Memory training is training in observation.

Our human powers of thought depend upon the symbolism of the word, and we think in words. That we cannot think except in words, as was contended by Max Müller, for instance, is not correct. We cannot think except in symbols, and other symbols, pictorial, auditory, tactual, may be used, as in all pre-linguistic stages they are, instead of words. Words are merely a much more efficient system of symbols, and they are used in thought with all the enhanced facility and economy which symbols afford, and also with the disadvantages which symbols entail. Like the mathematician who comes to lose sight of the meaning of the symbols which he combines, and is unable to interpret the symbolic result to which he is led, word-thought constantly becomes entangled in its own machinery of symbols, and brings forth into the world grotesque nonsense and verbal vacuities. The mass of mankind are ruled by the traditional, titular authority of words, and do not look beyond the consecrated symbol. Professor Ribot once made an interesting investigation into the representations spontaneously called up by abstract words. The results were in most cases ludicrous, even in people of the highest culture. With many the spoken word is found to awaken the mental presentation of its printed form. With others such a presentation is wholly absent, and difficult to call up, even intentionally ; the word-presentation is purely auditive. At its best in the trained mind abstract word-symbolism fulfils its function through the meaning of words having once been sufficiently investigated and pondered ; they thus become, like objects, complexes of varied values and utilitarian meanings, any particular aspect of which is called forth by the particular use to which they are put.

It is, in short, only the affective value, the use, the interest which in every case is reproduced ; when a purely cognitive value is represented it is by virtue of the fact that it has been observed in the light of a cognitive interest, has acquired a separate value of its own. We find it extremely difficult to compose a mental picture from a mere description, or even a graphic delineation, of unknown places, unknown people, when the sensory data of form, colour, etc., alone are supplied. Our reconstruction from such materials is, we find if we have the opportunity of checking it with the original, totally unlike the impression which we receive from the latter. The affective value, the emotional chord struck upon our conative appetences, our likes and dislikes, is the real fact of all experience. We can, or we imagine that we can, reconstruct the sensory experience from that ; but we cannot reverse the process and reconstruct an affective impression from merely sensory data. Hence the failure of art which is merely representative and accurate.

The actual world of experience is a world which affects us, an affective world, and one in which the possible reaction of that effect upon us, and our possible action upon it, are viewed. The illusion of a passively spectating organism bombarded by multifarious sensations and ' presented ' objects of knowledge is one that is created by the watchfulness of our organic sensory vedets. That conception, however, is that of the abstract philosopher, not that of the experient organism itself. For the latter the sensory world is still, as in its origin, the intentional discovery of an interested quest ; and only those constituents of it are noted whose relation, actual or symbolically significant, to conative tendencies bestows upon them a title to affective value.

Nor does it present itself as a mosaic of sensations ; the living organism cares nothing about sensations as such ; it cares about food, safety, pain, pleasure, it cares about the satisfaction of its conative dispositions and impulses. It cares about sensations, cognitively regarded, only in the capacity of signs, indications useful in relation to vital purposes. Only the philosopher analyses the external world into a world of sensations ; to the unsophisticated organism, to the questing animal, to the savage, to man when he does not don the attitude of the epistemolo gical philosopher, it is not a world of sensations at all, but a world of objects, of *things*. Those objects are not synthetized by the organism out of a bundle of sensations. These are but means which, having achieved their purpose, have no longer a value, an interest, and are discarded and disregarded. As once out of the undistinguished impinging affective ambient, the primitive organism picked out the sensory signs of discrimination, so in the developed sensory world the higher organism picks out objects which it does not analyse down into sensory constituents. Only as the need is imposed by interested motives does it perform that task of analysis and comparison, and dissociates differentiating qualities in the same way as the primitive organism compared one affective state with another, and dissociated distinguishing sensations. Objects and the qualities of objects are compared and judged.

To compare is necessarily to establish between objects a relation. Those relations are as real as that consistency of sensation which enables us to outline the possibilities of action in the external world ; it is the fragmentation of that world into objects, for our purposes and in our sense, which is arbitrary. That collection of objects is, in the human abstract intellect informed and quickened by a livelier notion of their relation through the concept of causation. Things are not merely compared as like and unlike, but as cause and effect. And the comparing intellect is raised to new powers of interpretation by that notion upon which all its reasoned constructions are founded.

Contemplated *logically*, the relation of cause and effect presents itself thus : (1) cause produces (2) effect. But that is not at all the psychological order. We do not go about stumbling upon causes, and thence proceed to inquire what effects those causes produce. That only occurs at most in experimental laboratories, which are quite a late development of human ingenuity. What we commonly do is the exact reverse ; we come upon effects and trace them to a cause ; a quite different process. And that is not a development of human ingenuity, but a process so ancient that its germ harks back, like that of all cognitive processes whatsoever, to the very first rudiments of sensation, and is implied in them.

Biologically considered, an effect is a *sign*. Sensation as distinguished from affection, serves the purpose of signifying something, something other than itself. A nidorous odour *signifies* the proximity of food. A sudden noise *signifies* the proximity of danger. The thing signified by the sensation is the *cause*. When a gazelle hears the roar of the lion, the effect, roar, is traced to its cause, lion, and is associated with it in experience. The roar is the effect of the lion, the lion is the cause of the roar. That is the original, biological prototype of the relation of causation, of the notion of cause. The cause is that which the effect signifies.

The relation is not in its essence and origin an intellectual process ; it is a crudely utilitarian, life-serving process. Life does not speculatively contemplate *rerum causas* ; it cunningly seizes upon every means of satisfying its impulses, of protecting itself ; and it overcame the disadvantages of waiting for a feeling which might prove its last, by forestalling it and detecting the signs of its approach. It discovered sensations significant of that proximate future ; and those sensations were the *effects* of causes.

To what manner of cause the effect is referred depends entirely upon the interest, the impulse by virtue of which that effect is noted. To the gazelle the roar of the lion, if associated with any representative idea at all, and not with a mere feeling of fear, will be associated with, referred to, the idea lion. The lion is the cause of the roar. It will not be referred to the vibrations of the air, or of the vocal cords in the lion's larynx, or to the nerve cells actuating those cords, or to Providence, or to ' Natural Selection.' The path along which an effect is traced to its cause is laid down by the interest of the individual, of his conative tendencies, in the situation. The cause of the effect is that for the sake of which the effect is noted in the service of its life-interests by the organism, as significant.

What is the cause of a given effect depends entirely on why we ask the question. Our notion that there are relations at all between things is but our way of putting the fact that there are no discreet things at all, that all things are parts or aspects of others. Our discrimination of experience into ' things ' is part of the cognitive process itself ; things are discriminated for the purposes of cognition. The notion that there can be entirely *different* things, separate ' substances,' is a fantasy the absurdity of which contradicts the very fact of cognition. There is no such thing as an object absolute and unrelated ; it is not the idea of relation which the intellect introduces into experience, but, on the contrary, it is the intellect's separations and distinctions, its creations of substantive and discreet objects, which is a utilitarian device of its cognitive operations. We cannot know without separating, distinguishing ; but that separation and distinction is merely a necessary method employed for the purpose of knowing, of comparing, of picking out signs from the external continuum. That continuum is restored by the third, the assimilating, grade of cognition, by relating every object to all others. In the physicist's conception of the universe, for instance, every atom is the resultant of all the forces in the universe ; separate the atom from the universe, nothing is left of the latter. Like the Leibnizian monad, every atom mirrors the whole universe. The path, therefore, along which we choose to trace the link of causation is entirely dependent upon our point of view. The linking up, like the differentiating, is a cognitive act, that is, the sign must correspond to that which it signifies, the association in thought must correspond to the association in experience ; else cognition fails to perform its function. To ascribe an effect to a cause which is not its invariable associate in experience is a fallacy of exactly the same nature as an illusion of the senses. To cognize for its life-serving purposes, the organism must pick out the sign which is empirically the invariable significant of a given situation or experience, the cause which is the empirical associate of the effect. It must not feel the sensation, or frame the explanation which it would like to be true, but that which is actually true, which corresponds to the empirical fact.

The feeling of power, of agency, experienced in the performance of our acts, to which all psychologists have traced the notion of cause, is but a quite secondary notion introduced at a much later biological date into the process. The agent, the efficient cause, is but a special case of the relation of sign and thing signified, effect and cause. One of the commonest interests by which man in a social state is prompted to trace an effect to its cause, a sign to the thing signified, is to discover ' Who did this ? ' The interest is in the human agent. And the human agent is picked out from among the multitude of causes of a given effect as the one with which we are concerned. There is, of course, a strong tendency in primitive psychology to extend the idea of human agency, to ascribe the thunderstorm, the flood, to a human agent. But it is untrue to say that the notion of agency is at the root of that of cause. Even in the most primitive and unsophisticated psychology it is not so. The savage may not only ask, ' Who did that ? ' but also ' How did he do that ? ' and ' Why did he do that ? ' Agency is but one mode of ' explanation.' We do not in thousands of cases think of a cause as an agent at all—when we ask why the sky is blue, why the earth is round, there is not a trace of the notion of agency in our concepts.

To trace an effect to its cause is not the discovery of an agent, but an *explanation* ; that is, a *comparison* between one sequence and another. Our need—originally, of course, our life-serving, utilitarian need—is satisfied when we have perceived the similarity between one chain of events and another ; that is all that any of our explanations can do ; never can they discover an agent. That subsumption, and not the discovery of an agent, is the utility of tracing a cause. When the movements of the moon are perceived to be similar to those of a falling apple, they are ' explained ' ; no agent has been discovered

in either case. The more sequences of events we perceive
to be similar, the more satisfied is our sense of explanation,
our knowledge of causes. If the likeness is found to
hold good in experience, if we can trust to finding always
similar sequences in the environment of similar events,
our explanation is true, just as our sensation is true if
it is invariably environed by similar experiences.

The notion of agency is only a special case of explanation.
We may explain motion in general by its similarity to
the motion to which we give rise. When our psychology
is confused and crude we shall say that things move because
they have thoughts, feelings, purposes ; when we perceive
that we may move without having thoughts, feelings,
purposes, and that those are only used by us to direct,
to serve our movements, that we move because we are
impelled to move, we shall say that things move because
they are impelled to move. We explain the impulse of
things to move by our impulse to move—or our impulse
to move by the impulse of things to move. For here we
reach a similarity the terms of which are mutually comparable, and not comparable to anything else ; to test
the truth of our comparison can only be done by reducing
the differences between our movements and the movements
of things to differences in the conditions and circumstances
in which those movements are produced. When we have
reduced all sequences of events to a fundamental similarity,
we are left with a sequence which we cannot compare
to anything else, which we cannot explain. We cannot
explain it by comparing it to a particular case of that
sequence itself, by comparing it to itself.

The function of cognition—here again including all
its forms from lowest to highest—is to set up a state
of belief. All life's dealings with the universe postulate
belief. The primordial and original attitude of all life
towards cognition is that of implicit belief. Primitive
animal life, protozoon or human baby, believes in the
edibility of everything ; the evolution of sensation is the

calling into doubt of that belief under the strokes of adverse experience. When a painful feeling is set up instead of a pleasant one, the reaction is inhibited, the organism doubts. Every step in the evolution of cognition has been the shattering of a belief, every discovery and development has been a disillusion. The progress of cognition has been the progress of doubt.

Every cognitive effort constitutes a 'conflict of motives,' a contest between opposite, contradictory impulses. The function of cognition is to inhibit the operation of incognizant appetence. The amœba that engulfs a flint instead of a diatom, the chick which desists from pecking orange peel that simulates yoke of egg, are being subjected to a 'conflict of motives.' The organism desires the pleasant, not the unpleasant, experience. The utility of the cognitive impulse, on the other hand, is to discern the signs of the actually impending experience, whether pleasant or unpleasant. In discharging that function it must do violence to the desire for satisfaction of another impulse ; it can only serve it by opposing it, by stifling it. The one impulse desires to find things as it wants them to be, the other as they are, as subsequent experience will prove them to be. All cognition is a contest between those two tendencies ; its function is fulfilled, or it is stultified and defeated at the cost and peril of the organism and of the race.

That conflict is the genetic mechanism of sensation ; it is also the theme of the evolution of human thought, of human belief. Here the conflict is magnified a thousand-fold.

Within the narrow range of primitive organic cognition, which does not extend beyond the immediate consequences of the moment, the castigating forces of instant experience compel the efficient operation of the cognitive function. The organism that should falsify its cognition by its desire for pleasant truth would at once perish. And sense-perception has become an automatic mechanism to be counted by a shallow analysis as a *datum* of experience.

In the work-a-day transactions of life man's cognition is likewise compelled to exercise its function, to be honest, to be, as we say, rational. But the opportunity for stultification increases with the scope of cognition. When that scope extends beyond the operation in individual experience of the chastening, compelling forces of immediate retribution ; when as a social being man deals with relations the bearing of which lies beyond the experience of the individual, in that of the race, with relations in dealing with which his cognitive faculty must rely for its validity upon the honesty with which it is exercised ; when it is checked only by racial, secular, indirect, not by immediate and individual consequences, he thinks that he is able to deceive himself with impunity.

Even greater obstacles than those arising from these intrinsic conditions militate in human society against the cognitive effort. Symbolic thoughts and concepts are transmitted socially ; and that heredity is not the product of a cognitive impulse, but of the interests of domination involved in the social conflict. The cognitive effort is not opposed by the individual's desire for falsehood alone, but by all the accumulated desires for falsehood of generations of established ruling powers, hedged with awful, sanctified values. The 'conflict of motives' assumes colossal proportions. The impulses which antagonize the cognitive effort are of such quality and power as almost to overwhelm it ; they do overwhelm it, so that a purely cognitive effort is for the individual well-nigh impossible. Only by a long-drawn racial, secular process, by the overtaking of lies by the Nemesis of their consequences in the racial evolution, can human cognitive power be set free.

The tribulations of human thought, the wars of opinions, the failures of metaphysics, of ethics, of politics, do not represent intrinsic disabilities of human thought—the fallibility of reason. To charge that intellectual and moral chaos to the imbecility of human cognition is a gross, fundamental, and cowardly misrepresentation, whereby human intelligence is made a scapegoat for the effects of the non-cognitive forces that have deliberately been employed in preventing its exercise. Human intelligence has not been confronted with riddles, so much as with lies. Its anarchy does not represent the fallibilities of its powers, but the defeat of those powers and their stultification in the conflict with non-cognitive impulses.

The impulse to cognition exists solely by virtue of its utilitarian life-serviceableness ; it is useful to the organism to discriminate between a diatom and a flint. If the desire to find a diatom where a flint is, overcomes the desire to discriminate between the two, the utilitarian function of cognition is abolished—at the cost of the organism. It is not from any incapacity to distinguish between diatoms and flints that human thought has suffered, but from the determination that flints shall be diatoms. That suicidal attitude—none the less fatal because it is on the racial rather than on the individual development that the scourge of its Nemesis falls—has been actually erected into a principle of wisdom. It has been thought that lies may be advantageous, expedient, beneficent, desirable. The plea is urged that it is advantageous to believe that flints are diatoms, that the object of cognition is the pleasantness of the result, as judged by the myopic standards of actuating interests. With blasphemous lack of faith, thinkers and philosophers have not shrunk from suggesting that *their* notion of fitness, and not the facts of the universe, are the standard of desirability and trustworthiness. The motive, the *vis a tergo* of their thought has not been a desire for truth, but a panic fear of truth, and they have undertaken the sacrilegious task of fitting on the frame of their Procrustean bed a bungled Universe, which, but for their orthopædic offices, were not decent to contemplate.

Human thought and human culture is at the present day paying the penalty—in its universal distrust, faithlessness, impotence, and Nihilism—of having lied to itself, of the supreme folly of imagining that it can become better adapted to the facts of life by trying to see them as they are not. Had we not for centuries devoted ourselves sedulously to extinguishing our eyes, to comforting ourselves by the discovery of agreeable truth, we should not at this stage be in need of comfort, of faith in life.

That doctrine of expedient falsehood—the head-fount of all human error, and consequently of all human suffering —arrayed in its latest garb as the fashionable thought-quackery of Pragmatism, insinuates itself—after the manner of ' Christian Science '—under the cloak of an indisputable truth : the functional nature of all cognition, the utilitarian function of all truth, and smuggles under that disguise the very poison that has paralysed those functions. We should like the object of cognition to be such and such, that it should be ' yoke of egg ' and not ' orange peel,' that the ' truth ' should be " attractive, valuable, satisfying " (F. C. S. Schiller). But by that very desire, the purpose for which cognition is sought, its utility to us, is defeated. By desiring the truth to be ' yoke of egg ' we shall presently get a horrible taste in our mouths. If our attitude were solely that of finding the sort of truth we wish to find, it would never be cognitive at all, and no cognitive impulse—the very reverse of that attitude—would ever have developed in the world. In order to exercise a cognitive function, in order to derive any advantage from the utility of cognition, we must do violence to our desire that its results shall be ' attractive, satisfying.' We must be prepared to cognize and accept the truth which is most atrociously unattractive and unsatisfying. We cannot cognize at all except at that price. The Pragmatist goes about whimpering that he is misunderstood, that his opponents are really Pragmatists at heart since they too acknowledge the functional nature of cognition. Precisely ; and it is in the name of that very function and utility which has been immemorially stultified by such quackery as the Pragmatist's, that they resist his juggling defeat of it. What the Pragmatist describes is not the function of cognition, but the pathological breakdown of that function. ' Truth is but the interesting expression of the amiable personality of the thinker.' Quite so, but the ' expression of personality ' which we find unamiable and perilous is the ' expression of the personality ' of a liar, especially if he be lying to himself. The ' expression of personality ' that is required is the expression of an *honest* personality, of one whose conception of truth is not that which he deems agreeable.

The ' fallibility of reason,' errors, illusions, inaccuracies, failures, mistakes, confusions, are not the things which are of real moment ; *they* rectify themselves soon enough by the natural selection of critical development. Not those ' fallibilities,' but the nature of the cognitive impulse which actuates the thinker and determines the process of his thought, is the thing which essentially matters.

' Methods ' for ' the conduct of the understanding,' ' logics,' are of comparatively small account. A great importance has been attached to them because it was unbeseeming and unpleasant to avow the real fountain head of truth and error. The notion has been cultivated that the advancement of correct belief depends upon the discovery of correct methods and ingenious ' logics.' Human intelligence can, as a matter of fact, be pretty well trusted to find its way to efficient methods of carrying out what it desires to carry out. That is a biological law. But the prerequisite for the operation of that law is that there should be a *desire,* a conative impulse, to use the available methods and instruments. Unless *that* is present, you may ' perfect your methods ' and construct as many systems of logic as you please, they will be all the more pernicious and misleading the more they are ' perfected.' Everyone imagines, of course, that he desires truth. The mystic, the champion of beseeming tradition and power-thought, will speak with as much conviction as anyone about his desire for truth. Here, then, we have a seemingly hopeless *impasse*, and there appears no escape from the personal view. But there is one test—Are you prepared to receive the truth that you most intensely *dislike*, the truth which in its whole significance is most abhorrent to you? That is the only Ithuriel's spear by which you may know whether you are capable of truth. The only ' method ' that matters is to reverse the Pragmatist's test. The only pernicious method is that of desiring ' agreeable ' truth.

What is an ' unpleasant ' truth? It is, in a broad biological sense, the truth to which we are not as yet adapted ; it is the truth that is too big for us, the truth up to which we have not grown, for which we are too little.

To straightforward cognition arising out of experience the notion of truth is in no doubt ; it is perfectly definite and simple. It is the fulfilment of the function of all cognition which only operates in order to discriminate in present experience the signs of an experience that is not present. It fulfils that function or fails to do so according as experience agrees or disagrees with the belief. If I say that there is a table in the next room, or that there are pyramids at Gizeh, the truth of my statement will be confirmed or confuted according as, on proceeding to the next room or to Gizeh, I shall find a table or pyramids. We need no metaphysical acumen to elucidate our notions of truth and falsehood, of validity or invalidity, in the beliefs we act upon, in all the concrete relations of life. To the youthful delinquent who is charged in connection with the disappearance of the jam from the pantry, jesting Pilate's question presents no riddle. He has a perfectly clear and definite notion of the difference between truth and a taradiddle. It is only by the woolly suggestion that Tommy's truth refers to one kind of veracity and Pilate's and the metaphysician's to another that a smoke-screen of confusion is cast about the latter.

The apparent difference is that some beliefs refer to matters that are at once directly checked by experience, and others to what lies beyond experience, and cannot therefore be checked. But no cognition, true or false, valid or invalid, transcends experience ; for no question can arise at all except *out of* experience, and the relation to experience which sets the question likewise checks the validity of the answer. The only difference is that the control of experience is exercised more or less directly, takes a longer or a shorter time to operate. Experience demands cash, or gives a short or a long credit ; but payment is invariably exacted. The longer the range of our questions, the more we are thrown back upon the accuracy of our thought ; our intellect is placed upon its honour. Our belief has a meaning or it has none, it is honest or it is dishonest. The meaning of a belief is either a presentation in terms of our experience, whether sensory or affective, whatever the postulated conditions of that experience ; or it is the apprehension of the inapplicability of those forms of our experience. But whatever differences of degree may obtain in the conditions of our cognition, those of our veracity remain unaltered. We think—the fancy has been sedulously encouraged—that we are at liberty to shape our ' truth ' as we please because no stern contradicting experience will pull us up and chastise us. *It will.* We or our children will be pulled up, will pay the full penalty of false cognition as surely and far more disastrously than if experience punished our self-deception by choking us on the spot. The consequences of Big Lies are exactly of the same kind as the consequences of little lies—they are found out.

And that is the great justification of our confidence in our powers of cognition. You think that you have demonstrated the ' fallibility of reason ' by showing that it can go wildly astray, and that there are things that we cannot know. You have done nothing of the sort. The function of cognition is not to know all, but to attain to accuracy in what it does know. And rational thought does, as a matter of fact, always sooner or later *find out lies*. The ' attractive, valuable, satisfying ' lie which you thought was quite safe because it dealt with matters ' beyond experience ' and could not be found out like Tommy's taradiddle, *is* found out nevertheless. ' Fallible ' human reason some day infallibly detects it. And the consequences of that detection are immeasurably more disastrous than the consequences of the detection of little lies. The world is sick to-day from nothing else than from the effects of ' attractive, valuable, satisfying ' lies. A fool's paradise may be ' attractive, valuable, satisfying '—for a time to the fool ; it is humanity at large that bears the brunt of the consequences.

That ineludible fate of all falsehood is the vindication of our cognitive powers. Those powers have operated despite all wills to falsehood ; they have, in spite of all, made for accuracy of thought. Metaphysical thought has in spite of itself carried out the process. The ' failure of metaphysics ' is essentially a misconception. I am one of the few who still believe in metaphysics ; for I do not see that metaphysical thought has ' failed.' I see, on the contrary, that it has steadily approached, not indeed to those goals of Unmeaning towards which it deliberately steered,[1] but, in spite of that fantastic steering, towards its only legitimate goal—accuracy of thought. That which is called the ' failure of metaphysics ' is, in fact, the exact opposite ; it is the success of metaphysics. Human thought has gradually purged itself into accuracy. Those things

---

[1] " Die unvermeindlichen Aufgaben der reinen Vernunft selbst sind Gott, Freiheit, und Unsterblichkeit. Die Wissenschaft aber, deren Endabsicht mit allen ihren Zerüstungen eigentlich nur auf die Auflösung derselben gerichtet ist, heisst Metaphysic."—*Kritik der reinen Vernunft*, Einleitung, iii.

which were once assumed postulates, unquestioned pre-conceptions, have become to every thinker untenable, negligible, and obsolete. The meshes of thought have been drawn closer and closer and alternatives eliminated. The 'failure of metaphysics' has brought about this result, that we know now pretty well the uses of our cognition.

That success of metaphysics is lamented as the demonstration of our ignorance. But it was, on the contrary, the grotesque incongruity of our pseudo-concepts which constituted our ignorance. What is left by their dissolution is not mere blank nescience, but the valid knowledge that the foundations of things are immeasurably greater than the pseudo-concepts and incongruities which we sought to substitute for their majesty.

CHAPTER V

ÆSTHETIC AND NOETIC ACTION

EVERY act of the organism modifies it. A portion of the configuration of its energy is destroyed, and is rebuilt slightly altered by the effect of each reaction. That modification has a physical aspect and a psychical counterpart. The organism is modified as a physical system, its structure is changed. The extent of that modification varies, for reactions frequently repeated, within wide limits, from unobservable molecular and metabolic changes to gross and visible molar changes. Thus the pseudopod of a protozoon becomes, if the organism remains fixed in one position, so that the same portion of its protoplasm is constantly used as a pseudopod, a permanent flagellum ; the sensitive protoplasm continuously reacting to light waves at the same spot becomes a pigment spot, the rudiment of an eye. The ' act ' becomes a ' structure.' That transformation of action into molar structure takes place most readily the simpler the organic form. Plants react by wholesale modification of their structure. Thus, transferred to a dry atmosphere the leaves of plants become converted into spines ; Alpine plants transplanted to a plain lose the squat, bunched and dwarfed appearance of mountain floras, and acquire long stems and elongated leaves ; watered with brine, inland plants acquire the peculiar characters of sea-shore plants ; and so forth. The ' intelligence of flowers ' takes the form not of acts, but of elaborate structures, such as those which excite our wonder and admiration in the devices of orchids.

Those structures are not, of course, the result of 'intelligence,' but the cumulative effects of the reactions of the organisms to conditions favouring or disfavouring their activities, aided by the action of natural selection. If those reactions have any psychical factor, it is not intelligence, or even sensation, or any cognitive process, but feeling in its original and most rudimentary form, the pure feeling of satisfaction or dissatisfaction.

There is, of course, no essential difference between big and small structure, between the most minute molecular modification and the development of a visible form or organ. Nor is there any sharp line of delimitation between act and structure, organ and function. Specialization of function, that is, the fixing of the type of reaction that has once taken place, and its facilitation by repetition, are physiological aspects of the modification of structure brought about as a necessary result of the repeated reactions of the organism. Not only is the structure of the individual organism modified, its conative dispositions are also modified ; they have assumed a determinate objective form, their general tendency has become a particular tendency, it has become directed to definite objects, so that a vague disposition to react to favourable circumstances has been converted into a specific disposition to react in a definite way to definite circumstances. That intimate conative change is not fixed in the individual only ; any portion separated from it that inherits the conative tendency which is the form of the organism's life, thereby necessarily inherits the same disposition to react to given conditions in the way established by previous reactions. The detached cell of a multicellular organism consisting of structuro-functionally differentiated cells, will, if it be itself sufficiently undifferentiated and unspecialized, reproduce the whole multicellular organism ; each daughter-cell reacting functionally and structurally to its relation to all others, in the same manner as the cells occupying corresponding positions, and having corresponding physiological relations, reacted in the parent organism. Thus the effects of every reaction, modifying as they do the structure and conative tendencies of the organism, tend to become fixed not only in the individual, but in the race. The fixation of organic reaction in permanently modified structure results in organized physiological function and reflex action—there is no essential distinction between the two—whereby a determinate reaction takes place automatically in response to the appropriate stimulus. Such a reaction approximates to our conception of a purely ' mechanical ' reaction, one which is unmodifiable by any psychological factor. And the reflex actions of organisms and tissues, of decapitated animals, and brainless frogs, were studied with great zest by Victorian science as links between inorganic mechanism and conscious behaviour. Reflex action afforded an example of action which, while rigidly and mechanically fixed in material structure, was yet ' purposive,' manifesting a clear relation to the interests of the organism. Hence its study proved highly interesting in the light of the ideal of deriving conscious action from that apparently pure mechanism.

Reflex mechanism is, of course, not the source, but the result of vital reaction. The mechanism which it most closely resembles is not an inorganic reaction, but a man-made machine, a mechanism into the structure of which a purpose has been introduced by the maker of the machine. And it is in that sense that reflex action is mechanical : it is machine-like ; the purposiveness is derived from its origin and is fixed in its structure. It was originally the ordinary reaction of the organism's conative disposition in response to a feeling of satisfaction or dissatisfaction, and the reaction has become consolidated in structure so as to operate in one fixed manner only. But it still differs in its mechanism from ordinary inorganic systems and man-made machines in being set in operation by a stimulus, that is, by the production of a feeling. We shall see that the absence of feeling from our conscious-

ness is no proof of the non-existence of the feeling. Apart
from that consideration we can satisfy ourselves in most
cases that reflex action takes place in response to a 'sensory'
(here meaning in reality an affective) stimulus. For
instance, one of the most obstinately operative of our
reflexes is the blinking reflex ; we are powerless to inhibit
it by any voluntary effort. Darwin relates how, while
observing a cobra, which dashed itself angrily against
the glass plate of its cage, he endeavoured to his utmost
power to inhibit his blinking reflex, but with no success.
But now try to produce the blinking reflex in a new-born
child. You cannot. That obstinate mechanical reflex
which even the mind of Darwin is unable to control,
cannot take place when a 'stimulus,' though physically
impressive, is not perceived, has no affective value. The
machine-like operation which was brought into existence
by the operation of feeling still requires some form of
feeling to set it working.

While the attempt to derive adaptive action proper from
'mechanical' reflex was an inversion of the sequence
obviously indicated by all observation as well as by logic,
some confusion is liable to arise in the opposite direction
from our common experience that purposive effort passes
with us into subconscious automatism, as when we learn
to walk, skate, swim, write, ride a bicycle, etc. Here
the purposiveness and effort are in the first instance
elaborate, and this conversion of an elaborate purposiveness into a mechanism suggests a similarly elaborate
psychological origin of organic reflexes in general. The
analogy is misleading. That elaborate purposive education
does not exist except in the most highly developed forms
of life. The type of reaction which has given rise to most
organic reflexes is the original type of vital reaction.
And that has nothing to do with cognition in any form
or with a cognized purpose ; it is simply the reaction
to the pleasant or unpleasant feeling produced by a given
activity.

The development of behaviour has taken place according to two distinct types or methods of action. In the first, actions are governed by feeling alone. They have no conscious purpose beyond that immediately represented by that feeling itself at the moment. To that type of reaction the name of *æsthetic action* may be given. In the second type the immediate feeling is not the sole conscious determinant, and the act itself is a step in a chain of behaviour leading to a prospective result. It is performed in view of that ulterior inducement. Such an act involves cognition ; the act is performed as a conscious means to an end. We may call such a mode of action *noetic action.*

In reflex action a specific act in response to a given feeling is fixed in the individual and in the race, just as a feature, a mannerism, a taste for a particular kind of food, are fixed in organic constitution and in heredity. That fixation of reaction extends much farther than a single reaction, in the same way as the fixation of structural characters extends much farther than a single ' character.' All the structural characters of an organism of extremely complex structure and specialized differentiations are, we know, thus fixed in the reaction of each of its constituent cells. In suitable conditions one of those cells, being undifferentiated for any local function, and consequently retaining all its powers of growth (germ cell), will multiply ; and its daughter-cells will, step by step, differentiate themselves from one another, assuming specialized functions according to their relation to other cells and to the whole, and so go through the apparently marvellous process of building up by stages the entire organism anew with all its ' characters,' its tricks of manner, and all. It is as merely puerile to imagine, as so many of our biologists have, under the influence of Weismannian mythology, been employed in doing, that each ' character ' —whatever that may be—is represented by the tessera of a mosaic, as it would be to ascribe each of the possible reactions of a carbon molecule to a separate 'gemmule' of reaction, or the various properties of a sphere to a corresponding number of 'biophores.' The form of the conative disposition of every cell in the body being once modified, its reactions to every possible relation are thereby modified; and every embryonic cell endowed with the same character must of necessity, in identical physiological circumstances, reproduce the differentiations of corresponding cells in the parent organism which occupy the same positional and functional relation to the whole and to the environment.

That reproduction of reaction-values does not by any means end with embryological development; it continues in precisely the same manner throughout the life of the organism. Structure and behaviour are, I repeat, but formal and superficial distinctions. Just as the character of the conative energy common to all the cells of a multi-cellular organism (apart from their local functional differentiation) reproduces the bodily growth of their ancestry, so it in the same manner reproduces the behaviour of that ancestry.

Thus not only is every single act fixed, to a greater or less extent in structure and in conative disposition, but entire courses of conduct, entire modes of life, chains of processes of any degree of elaboration, such as nest or comb-building, community organization, and so forth. That reproduction of behaviour, identical in its causation with the reproduction of structural organization, is what is spoken of as instinct.

The word once stood for one of the mysteries of Christian philosophy, being the endowment bestowed by the Creator on the beasts that perish, as the 'rational soul' was bestowed on man. Far from being a special endowment, it is the primitive, straightforward operation of the constitution of living organization, whereby life endures apart from the individual, perpetuates itself. The results of its reactions must, in order to that continuity, be in some manner fixed, transmitted. And that fixation takes place automatically as a consequence of the modification brought about by every act in the system of energy whence it derives. Every reaction tends to become fixed both in the organism and in the race ; every successive life tends to reproduce both the organism and its behaviour with stereotypical fidelity. The logical outcome of the fundamental properties of living organization would be the perpetual repetition in every detail of the individual life. It is the breaking away from that process, it is variation, and the noetic type of action among other things, that constitute special afterthoughts in the methods of life.

You are puzzled by the purposiveness and the elaborate nature of some animal instincts. ' Purposive ' every vital reaction is, inasmuch as it is the satisfaction of an impulse, but the teleology of instinct is represented in consciousness by feeling only, by likes and dislikes. Instinctive behaviour is purely æsthetic behaviour. The organism is instigated to a course of action by the attractiveness to him of those actions and of the objects connected with them, without any consciousness whatever of their utility, without any perception of purpose. Why does a hen sit on eggs ? why do wasps build mud-nests ? Because they *like* to. There is no more to be said about it, so far as the consciousness of the instinctive organism is concerned, than about your liking for oysters or for neutral tints. *De gustibus.* . . . The mode of operation of instinct is clearly illustrated in the *playful* activities, the apparently objectless activities of the young. Play is essentially the manifestation of instinct in the absence of its object. The kitten that has never seen a mouse, or maybe another cat, will chase imaginary mice and play with balls of cotton in the traditional racial manner of dealing with mice. The pup will tear and gnaw, track and explore. The young human male will play at building things, at soldiers, at Red Indians, at pirates ; the young human female will play with dolls. Those activities are attractive, amusing, engrossing. All amusement, all play, all tastes, are manifestations of instincts, in appearance a purposeless exuberance of energy, in their vital significance deeply teleological. The bird plays at nest-building with as intense an earnestness as the little girl plays with her doll. The mason-wasp amuses itself by deftly paralysing caterpillars and sealing them in its mud-nest, where they will serve as food for larvæ of which she knows nothing and that she will never see. In very much the same way—with just a little more play of consciousness about the act—the dying man who knows that he has not six months to live, will be impelled to marry the woman he loves, or to give utterance to the ' message ' that is in him. They like to do so ; it gives them satisfaction to do those things, just as it gives them satisfaction to eat. ' They,' man, bee, or wasp, are nothing but the conative impulses of the life-force which tends towards goals unrepresented in their consciousness, and which is transmuted into intense desires and pleasures by any reaction which serves its ' purpose.'

The tastes of the bee, the wasp, the sacred beetle, are odd, concerned with peculiar, very specialized objects. The more primitive, the more lowly, the grade of development of life's activities, as in the ' physiological ' acts of our living tissues, the more ' odd,' that is, specialized, are the objects with which they are concerned, the narrower the compass of those activities. Bees have become concerned with a particular ' line ' of activities having to do with nectar, wax, combs, hive-organization ; and their fixed activities have developed into elaborate, minute, finicking details concerning that particular ' line.' Once specialization has taken place, development can only accumulate detail upon detail within the sphere of that specialization ; the whole conative impulse of life is confined and imprisoned within it. In like manner a human community to whom money has come to be the means to everything, will in time come to think economically, to formulate all the values of life in terms of pounds, shillings, and pence. All specialization narrows and confines the range of activity, and elaborates it within that range; development proceeds from without inwards, and cannot expand.

That original method of fixation which reaches its highest perfection in insects, in whom we admire the wonders of instinct, has its advantages and disadvantages. It greatly simplifies and economizes individual action. A whole elaborate course of life is supplied ready-made, as it were, to the individual; there is no occasion for tentative effort, there is no room for doubts and hesitations. For the organism there is between such a fixed, ready-made behaviour and the tentative determination of conduct the same difference in simplicity and economy of individual effort and development as there is between turning the handle of a gramophone and playing a violin. The conduct of the living organism is already registered and stereotyped on the plate of his nervous gramophone. He has but to be wound up, and the behaviour is ' paid out ' automatically. Further, the mechanism can be indefinitely multiplied and reproduced wholesale in its most complex and perfected form, so that every individual of the race can ply his gramophone, and each stands at the same level as the most efficient performer; whereas the violin can only be played satisfactorily by the most gifted and highly trained individuals. On the gramophone system of behaviour every performer is raised by heredity to the level of a Paganini, whereas the violin system establishes differences between individuals. The one system is perfectly equalitarian, levelling all habilities, the other is an inevitable source of inequality.

Against those great advantages there are, however, serious disadvantages to be set down. The stereotyped conduct, however complexly perfect, clearly places the organism at a disadvantage when dealing with new conditions. The elaborate perfection of its automatism is acquired at the price of a loss in flexibility. The greater the elaboration, the greater the fixity and rigidity; so that ultimately the possibilities of further development become entirely excluded. Your gramophone-playing race ceases to produce Paganinis. The path of development, which proceeds from without inwards by greater and greater elaboration of detail within a determined sphere, ends at last in a *cul-de-sac*. Evolution must become completely arrested.

The fixation of conduct in instinct was the path of least resistance in the course of evolution. And it produced that marvel of insect behaviour which is so elaborate and so perfect that many people have even expressed doubts as to whether it is not superior to human methods of conduct; and the perfect organization, balanced adjustment, and smooth working of insect communities, are constantly held up as patterns and models to human communities.

There was a stage in the course of organic evolution when the class of insects was the crowning top of that process. Had there been an insect philosopher at the time, he would have had no difficulty in showing how the marvellous achievements and powers of the insect soul were the predestined goal towards which all the process of evolution had from the age of the nebula been tending. To produce a community of bees might well be, he would delicately suggest, the very *Telos* of the universe, the realization of that far-off, Divine event to which the whole creation moves. There existed a number of other forms of life in which the process of fixation of behaviour, the accurate transmission of elaborated courses of conduct in the form of solidly constructed, firmly stable mechanisms, had not proceeded in the same way as in insects. They were clearly unsuccessful, inferior forms, they were obvious failures, hopelessly outclassed and outstripped in the race of development.

Strange irony! It was precisely in those failures, in those unsuccessful forms of life, that the future of organic evolution lay. The descendants of those outdistanced backward races were destined to bruise the insect under their heels. They were lacking in the power of firmly and solidly organizing their nervous substance in a broad-based, efficient stable manner. Their activities were not concentrated on one particular speciality of behaviour. They were anarchic, disorderly persons, who had a natural incapacity for the arts of stable government; they could not produce a perfect machine, so perfect as to be, like the British Constitution, insusceptible of improvement. They went about their business in an haphazard sort of way, now acting in one fashion, now in another, unable to make up their minds, having constant revolutions and changes of policy. The insect philosopher, I have no doubt, published a book pointing to them as fearful examples, as inferior races, who did not know how to behave, and even advocating the duty, the obligation incumbent on sensibly organized insects to put a stop to the nuisance of those wild people, and to all that experimenting in behaviour, which was utterly disgraceful, and might even in time have a demoralizing influence on soundly, rightly thinking insects.

I apologize for the flippancy. The allusiveness of our insect philosopher is not, however, wholly irrelevant. Life's facts are very broad. In human development as in organic evolution, in human as in biological affairs, the contests of the self-same forces are at work, the contests between stability and instability, change and conservation, preservation and development, specialization and experiment. And we have the paradox that in all evolution the main line of progress runs through the apparent failures, and leaves apparent success stranded in backwaters. Achievement tends to arrest; it is the less perfected, the less settled organization that is predestined to ultimate success.

It is by the development of cognition, of noetic reaction, that behaviour has broken through the iron circle of fixed hereditary instinct. That fixity was the outcome of reaction to feeling. The organism that reacts solely to the affective value of the moment will react in exactly the same way to its repetition ; and feeling and reaction are stamped for ever in hereditary structure. Behaviour is thus fixed in an eternal recurrence. Feeling is the conservative principle of psychical causation. The behaviour that is governed by feeling, by emotion, by sentiment, is the conservative type of behaviour—the female, the religious type.

Cognition, on the other hand, is intransmissible. Powers and instruments of cognition can be handed down by heredity, but not their products. No organism is born with inherited sensations, presentations, ideas, knowledge. Those it can only acquire through individual development. With noetic behaviour the possibilities of life, the building up of behaviour, begin anew in each individual. Each situation must be dealt with on its own merits. An individual instead of a racial memory, a presentative memory instead of a motor and structural one, is constructed.

Pure feeling, the original sole determinant of behaviour, is bound to the present instant, to the actual moment. Æsthetic reaction is entirely comprised within that present. All presentation, all cognition, is the protension in time of the determinants of action. In the simplest cognitive operation, in sensation, however rudimentary, the present expands into the past and the future. In the discriminative sensory exploration an unsatisfied conative impulse tends towards a satisfaction which is deferred ; it looks forward into the future, is a means to an end ; and it compares the actual by looking back upon a past experience, by reproducing a previous affective attitude. In it are all the rudiments of desire, of memory, and of purpose.

The development of cognition is the expansion into

wider and wider reaches of time of the determinants that
shape the organism's reaction to the actual present. The
cognizing organism does not react to the present merely,
but to a feeling which it forestalls. It foresees an
impending future feeling ; it has therefore time to use
the intervening conditions as values related to that foreseen feeling, to that hope or fear : a new range of values
is thus opened to individual cognition.

The behaviour of the purely æsthetic organism may be
elaborately teleological through the gradual building up
step by step of complex chains of action, each phase of
which calls forth the next by making it desirable to the
organism. But the conscious ' motive ' consists solely in
the affective value, in the attractiveness of that immediate
step, and that is as rigidly fixed in racial memory, as
fatally determined as the end of the process. The æsthetic
organism is essentially an automaton. In noetic action
the end may be as fixed in hereditary determination as
it is in the æsthetic organism, but the path of ways and
means that lead up to it remains labile and is not consequent upon inherited æsthetic reactions, but on the
individual cognitive powers, the operation of which can
bring to light new forms of feeling, new values, new
actualizations of its conative dispositions. Thus is the
development of conation possible only in the cognizing
organism. Only through the play of increasing ranges of
cognition can the original drive of the conative forces of
life work their way to greater and greater self-realization
awakening to new possibilities as they strike out new paths
of action. Only through cognition is their development
possible.

Nowhere, above the most primitive phases, is absolutely
pure æsthetic reaction to be found ; nowhere certainly
purely noetic action. Some latitude of modification is
permitted even in the most closely organized instincts.
When the object of desire fixed in the instinct is not
available, the nearest substitute becomes an object of

fascination. Thus birds that are in the habit of building on ledges of rock will adapt themselves to the eaves of houses, and vice versa. The mason-wasp itself, the classic of elaborate fixed instinct, has acquired in New Zealand a taste for spiders instead of caterpillars, the latter being unavailable. And, while noetic action operates in conjunction with the most complex instinctive behaviour in birds and mammals—as in the building instincts of birds, of beavers—instinct, on the other hand, the hereditary transmission of æsthetic reaction, the direct and primitive method of determination of animal behaviour, continues to be operative, constitutes indeed the foundation and the bulk of all behaviour, even where cognition and its operation on action reach their highest development, in man himself.

The discovery that the soul of man is compounded of instincts has rightly been counted the greatest advance ever made in psychological science—the first glimpse, properly speaking, of the reality of things in regard to that. The old fantastic mythologies which pictured animals as ' endowed ' with instinct, and man as ' endowed ' with a ' rational soul,' have lapsed into the limbo of fables.

In the psychic structure of man we see, as it were in a geological stratification, every successive form of vital reaction represented. His ' physiological ' functions operate in a fixed mechanism of reaction ; his cells busy themselves with their chemical operations, respirations and absorptions, like those of plants and marine protozoa. They reproduce his organism in successive stages by an elaborate series of co-ordinated reactions, a fixed chain of conduct. Motor, secretory acts of varying complexity are rigidly fixed in the structure of his tissues as reflex arcs ; some quite uncontrollable in their action, others amenable in varying degrees to influences from other parts of his organism. Appetences and repugnances hereditarily established give rise to instinctive acts identical with those of other animals. The young human seeks his mother's nipple by virtue of an instinct as old as the earliest mammal, manifests his needs by vociferous cries, and presently attempts to crawl and eventually to stand on his hind-limbs. He is terrified at objects and sounds to which affective evolution has assigned values evocative of the instinct of fear, and seeks other objects that have become bound up with feelings of delight and desire ; he is sickened and disgusted, excited and exalted, by virtue of ancestral sentiments ; explores his environment instigated by an inherited protective and acquisitive instinct of curiosity ; becomes angry and pugnacious in response to the stimulus of situations which ancestral experience has marked as favourable to the exercise of his terror-inspiring influence upon others ; displays the humility of the weak before the strong, the vain self-display of the male, the cunning wiles of the female, and glows with the poetry of life under the blind primary urge of her impulse to perpetuation. The great bulk of the ' motives ' which prescribe his conduct are instinctive impulses once acquired by his ancestry and fixed in his organism ; he reproduces in his conduct and demeanour the decisions laid down by primordial vegetable cellules, by protozoan animalcules, by worms and reptiles, by forgotten generations of his own race, by every forbear of his motley geniture. And where he most originally, cunningly or sublimely manifests himself in his deepest wisdom and most soaring aspirations and ideals, he is still giving expression to the constituent conative dispositions of all life, whose ultimate significance are as invisible, as unknown, as unintelligible to him, as were to the infusorian and the worm the instincts which they have transmitted to him.

A very different purview from that which we were wont to contemplate in the separate universe of the human soul ! But in the first flush of the discovery certain proportions are liable to be overlooked, with misleading effect. The operation of psychic forces is fundamentally identical throughout the course of life, from the first amœboid jelly to man himself. But that unity lies in the continuity of the evolutionary process, and it behoves us to perceive, besides that unity, the unfolding development which is the essence of that process, to apprehend wherein its highest products differ from its inceptions, its mature fruit from its germ. When, in contrast with the fabulous psychologies of yore, the truth is flashed upon us that there is no disparity, no contrast, no breach in the continuity of all animal activity and of our own, we proclaim the new-found truth by saying that ' Man is a creature of instinct.' That is strictly and wholly true. But when, setting aside the controversial emphasis of the contrast with old fables which that truth supplants, we regard the process of psychic evolution itself, and compare human psychism with that out of which it has grown ; when from that point of view we say ' Man is a creature of instinct,' the statement, while remaining true, becomes misleading. It leaves out of sight the fact that the distinctive character of human psychism is precisely that the part of instinct is here reduced to smaller dimensions than in any other organism. The distinctive trait of human psychism, as compared with that of other animals, is the surpassing of instinct. Man is the *least* instinctive of any animal. Not the instinctiveness of his behaviour, but the relative independence of instinct which he has achieved, is the characteristic of human behaviour.

He is a compound of instincts, but none of those instincts is the elaborate specialization of a given oddity of life-pursuit ; he has inherited no comb-building, or migratory instincts, no hard and fast social organization. He is no bee, no wasp. He is the heir of those organic forms that have kept instinct generalized by introducing in its operation the control of cognition. Between the instant situation and the goal of feeling there has become intercalated in human ancestry a cognitive process of presentative values which, like a wedge, has gradually widened the gap between the two ; and that interspace, instead of being filled in with a chain of æsthetic reactions stamped irretrievably in racial structure, has developed into ever farther-reaching previsions and retrospects, with devisings of ways and means. These are the domain of the individual life, and are insusceptible of being fixed or transmitted in hereditary structure.

Noetic action has culminated in the powers of the symbolism of conceptual thought. The conative impulses of life, hitherto groping in narrow channels of affective response, found the way open to their actualization in a manner never before possible. And in proportion as man uses those cognitive powers is his control extended —' his control,' that is to say the self-realization of the *primum mobile* which actuates him.

CHAPTER VI

THE ORGANISM AND FOCAL CONSCIOUSNESS

ONE great disadvantage that besets our study of conscious psychism is that the only specimen available to direct observation is the most complex and elaborate under the sun. We are in very much the same position in our investigation of psychological dynamics as we should be if we set about the study of physical dynamics and, knowing nothing of the simpler kinds of machines, such as a lever, a wheel, a crank, were compelled to begin our enquiry into mechanical principles by considering, say, a great newspaper printing-machine whirling at high speed, with all its cylinders, cog-wheels, tubular plates, shafts and cranks in rapid and complex motion, and we were to endeavour to formulate our notions of mechanical principles from that. You may well imagine how unsatisfactory the progress of our science of mechanics would be under those circumstances, and how long it would take us to discover, for instance, the simple laws of motion formulated by Galilei and Newton. The extremely complex, composite nature of the only form of psychic machine known to us by direct experience constitutes a serious handicap, and renders us naturally liable to mistake the superficial and incidental for the essential and fundamental, a type of error with which all our psychology is deeply fraught.

Hence it is that in order to understand the essential and fundamental features of the operation of psychic act on we have been obliged to refer constantly to organic systems of energy reduced to their simplest expression, and to follow those psychic processes not in the soul of man only, but in that of the most rudimentary and primitive organisms, of protozoa, such as the familiar amœba. If it be objected that we can know nothing directly of the amœba's soul, the reply is that we can study at our leisure its behaviour, and that is one of the most reliable data of psychology. A great part of our psychological knowledge is derived from our observation of the behaviour of others, and we can study that much more conveniently in the amœba than in our friends.

The amœba has no brain or nervous system, it has no limbs, no stomach, no lungs, no liver, no heart, no kidneys. It is, however, a very remarkable and significant fact that, although the amœba is entirely destitute of all those organs, it does essentially everything that other animals, including ourselves, do with the whole apparatus of nervous system, limbs, viscera, etc. It breathes as well as you or I, it breathes with its whole body ; it puts forth its protoplasm and makes very efficient temporary limbs out of it, pseudopods, with which it crawls about and seizes its prey as effectually as the lion seizes his. It encloses it in a hollow space contrived for the purpose in its protoplasm, and proceeds to secrete hydrochloric acid and peptic juices, and to digest its dinner much better than many of us who have to be careful about our diet and swallow pepsin tablets. It excretes urea as well as if it had the most healthy kidneys. It can be quite wide awake and react as infallibly to an external event as if it were a mass of nerves ; and when it has had a good dinner it curls itself up into a ball and sleeps the sleep of the just. Although it has no eyes, its whole body is keenly sensitive to changes of light. It reproduces its kind by using its whole body as a germ. You adduce the heroic paradoxes of human conduct, the supreme sacrifice of the martyr. Well, the amœba too can play the martyr. It can sever its body into two— a most uncomfortable procedure, I should fancy. Perhaps it likes it ; the martyr too, if it comes to that, ' likes ' his martyrdom, or he would not accept it. The amœba commits hari-kiri impelled by certain impulses which transcend individual appetites.

Rather than say that our amœba has no nerves, limbs, stomach, etc., it would be considerably more correct to say that it is all nerves, limbs, stomach, all eyes, all lungs. There is in truth not a single act of life, not a single physiological function that you can name, which our most elaborate organism performs, that is not also performed, in its essentials, by the single-celled amœba. That is a most significant and momentous fact. What then is evolution ? We have been so filled with wonder at the marvellous building up of an innumerable variety of new forms from one another, at the coming out of a whole Noah's ark out of that miserable little speck of primordial protoplasm, at the wonders that issued from such humble beginnings, that we had some difficulty in crediting them. And when we come to look into the matter, lo ! nothing new has really been produced. We find at the very beginning of life essentially everything that can be discovered in its crowning achievement. Evolution has created nothing. Professor Bergson enthusiastically calls it ' Creative Evolution,' but of creation— in the proper sense of the word, the producing of something that was not there before, something entirely new —there is not a trace.

The essential process of all the activities and behaviours of life is, we have seen, the satisfaction of its conative dispositions under the guidance of feeling. That is done by the amœba, and nothing more is ever done by man. What has been developed, what has been perfected, what has been evolved, is purely and solely the means of carrying out that reaction. Throughout the phases and forms of organic life the disposition of energy remains the same, the tendencies of its reactions remain the same, the essential relation of those inherent dispositions to ambient conditions remains the same, the direction of life's impulses remains the same.

From a biological point of view there is, fundamentally considered, but one animal—the protozoon. The single-celled organism is properly the only existing system of living energy. All other organic forms, the ' higher animals,' man himself, are but combinations, aggregates of protozoa. And all the developments of means and powers, all the ' faculties ' of higher animals and man, are but quantitative modifications and combinations of the functions and reactions of protozoic cells. Out of the original protozoa all animal and human organization has arisen, and every individual life arises likewise out of a single protozoic cell.

The human organism consists, it is estimated, of something like twenty-six and a half billions of cells, the progeny of the protozoic germ-cell. Of these, however, some sixteen and a half billions are but carriers of oxygen—the red blood cells—and are probably not to be regarded as living cellular entities, but as dead cells utilized for that mechanical function. So that the number of living cells in the human organism may be set down at about ten billions (10,000,000,000,000). Each of those cells is absolutely analogous to, and many are quite undistinguishable from, various forms of protozoa which live an individual life as separate organisms. Thus the white cells of the blood are identical in structure and behaviour with amœbæ ; unstriped muscle-cells are exactly similar to gregarinæ ; the columnar and ciliated cells of the alimentary canal, respiratory tract and Fallopian tubes, to vorticellæ or pintinni and to colpodian parasites ; nerve-cells, the cells of the cerebral cortex, are almost identical with rhizopods, such as *gromia, chlamydomyxa, actinophrys*, and other animalcules. There is no cell in the human organism that cannot be almost exactly matched with some form of independent unicellular organism.

The powers and faculties of the human organism as a whole differ from those of an isolated protozoon only as the powers of a highly trained and efficiently organized army or community differ from those of their individual component taken severally. The higher efficiency of the organized whole depends upon the coordination of the activities of its constituent members ; but nothing is superadded to those powers.

Organic coordination is the effect of structural and functional differentiation and specialization. It is of the first importance, if we would gain an adequate conception of the operation of the complex organism and of its psychical activities, to understand what is implied by that differentiation and specialization. And in order to do so we must endeavour, first of all, to dismiss from our minds the notion that ' hierarchies,' distinctions between ' ruling ' and ' servile ' elements, have any place in the organization of the living body. Anthropomorphizing imagination has, from the time of Plato, imported the vices of human social organization into physiology, in the same manner as it has imported them into cosmology, building its conception of the universe after the model of an Oriental satrapy, or savage patriarchy. Contemporary physiology is still permeated with such superstitions. We may be confidently assured that nothing of the nature of such human stupidities and iniquities are to be thought of in connection with the organization of any part of the natural order.

Free protozoa become, like all other living things, modified in structure and function in relation to their environment and mode of life. The component cells of a metazoic organism likewise become differentiated in relation to their environment in the compound organism, and to the mode of life consequent upon those relational conditions. Cells are specialized so as to perform particular functions ; some are particularly developed in the direction of secretion, others in that of motility, others in that of particular forms of sensory cognition, and so forth. But it must not be supposed that, while organic elements are thus specialized, and devote the greater part of their energy to one particular form of vital activity, they do not at the same time retain and fulfil every function common to all living organisms. Though the intestinal cell is specialized for absorption, and the muscular cell for contractility, yet the intestinal cell continues to be contractile and the muscular cell absorbent. Specialization is never complete ; every living cell performs *all* the functions of life. Specialization involves no *new* form of activity, and the specialized cell acquires no power which it did not possess before. The modifications which constitute specialization are quantitative, not qualitative ; a cell specialized for a given function develops one of the aspects of its activity in a given direction, but it acquires no new function, nor does it cease to perform any of the functions of life which it previously exercised.

The activities of our organisms are no more sharply divided into ' functions ' than our mental activities are divided into ' faculties.' Our physiology to which the elementary and fundamental laws of vital action are as yet entirely unknown, is a sort of ' faculty physiology,' which divides the body into ' systems '—the respiratory system, the alimentary system, the genito-urinary system, and so forth. No ' system ' has an independent function ; its ' function ' is a resultant of the activity of all other ' systems.' The operation of the central nervous system is indissolubly linked with exchanges of gases, digestive and assimilative processes, excretory processes, secretory processes, reproductive processes ; it performs each and all of those ' functions ' in addition to those which constitute its specialized activity. And, on the other hand, every element in the body, no matter what its specialized activity may be, performs in some form those functions which are specialized in the central nervous system.

If two living cells are in organic continuity with one

another, through even the finest thread of living substance, the reaction of both cells will be absolutely identical. Thus when a vegetable cell connected to another by a long protoplasmic filament of extreme tenuity, sets about secreting a cell-membrane, the second cell, even if enucleated, will do likewise and will continue to do so as long as the connection is intact.[1] As long as two protozoa (*Stentor*) remain connected by a strand of protoplasm, all their movements will be identical in the minutest detail ; all their cilia will vibrate in exact unison, bending in the same direction at the same instant.[2] The simplest multicellular organism is a mere hollow ball of flagellated cells, *Volvox* ; there are, of course, no controlling or integrating centres ; but each flagellum moves in exact unison with all the others, so that the organism spins round in a perpetual rotation.   In fine, the conative dispositions, even if different, of two cells that are in organic continuity assume the equilibrium of a common conative disposition which is the resultant of the two.   The determining principle of the activity of two such cells is equilibrated to a common level, like water in two communicating vessels ; so that every detail of their reaction and behaviour is absolutely identical in both cells, *provided the conditions of the environment are substantially the same for both cells.*

But suppose now that the conditions of the environment are different for each of the two cells organically connected. Let one be situated on the external surface (ectoderm) of a hydroid polyp, and the other on the internal surface of its enteric cavity (endoderm).   Both cells are in organic continuity, and by the above Law of Equilibrium their conative dispositions are identical ; but their functional behaviour will be different because their external and internal relations are different.   The external cell is in relation to the surrounding water, and will have to seek its food out of it ; the internal cell is in relation with

[1] C. O. Townsend, *Jahrb. wiss. Botanik*, xxx, 1897.
[2] A. Gruber, *Ber. Naturfor. Ges.*, Freiburg, iii.

the sack-like internal cavity into which food is swallowed, and is concerned with the digestion and absorption of that food. Their situations are different ; and the effect of the common conative disposition of the two cells is to cause them, not to do the same thing, but to do *what the other would do if it were in the same situation*. Both cells have a common tendency, equal reaction-values, identical interests ; hence the teleology of their reactions is directed, *mutatis mutandis*, according to the diversity of their situations, to the satisfaction of that common interest. The ectodermal cell does not capture food and retain it, but drives it into the digestive cavity ; the endodermal cell does not assimilate the whole of the food thus obtained by their joint action, but transmits, after digestion, a portion of it to the ectodermal cell by means of the fluids which bathe its external surface. The equilibrium of the conative disposition of the two cells results in an accurate division of labour, a perfect correlation between the activities of the two. There is here no ' higher control,' there are no ' ruling cells ' ; there is no integrative nervous system in the polyp.

In that equilibrium of the conative dispositions of living cells organically connected, varied in its manifestations according to the diversity of internal and external relations, we have, I believe, the entire *modus operandi* of metazoic organization, and of those infinitely minute and unfailing adjustments and integrations of complex coordination, which surviving conceptions drawn from mythological similitudes with barbaric states so signally fail to elucidate.

The reaction of every system of energy is a function of two factors, the disposition of the system itself and that of the ambient conditions which call forth its reaction. The first of those factors is a constant for every element of the organism, the second is a variable depending upon the total relations of the part. The modification brought about by each reaction in the uniform factor gives rise in turn to a modification of that factor in every part of the organism, every element of which is modified by each reaction of every other element.

All the cells of a multicellular organism are organically continuous. They are, as are likewise the embryonic cells of the developing organism, connected one with another by numerous intercellular bridges of protoplasm. In higher organisms those connections are supplemented and simplified by nerve connections.

It is not, however, the function of the central nervous system of the vertebrates to establish such a connection ; it is with the sensory and molar motor functions of the organism that it is primarily concerned, and its distribution to the skeletal muscles and to the organs of special sense are adapted to that function of sensori-motor coordination. With the viscera the connections of the central nervous system are indirect, nor do they appear to carry any direct motor or sensory impulses. The sympathetic system, on the other hand, is very differently distributed. It has no exclusive sphere ; wherever the finest capillary vessel penetrates to support cell nutrition a sympathetic fibre accompanies it. In it we have a complete network of intercommunication between all the elements of the body, and further an open channel of intercourse, through the white and grey communicating branches, between each and all parts and the central nervous system. There is no indication of any centralization of function in the sympathetic itself.

Section of the sympathetic in the neck causes dilatation of the blood-vessels, increased tone in the muscles, increased nutrition and keenness of sensation. Galvanic stimulation of its fibres gives rise to the opposite effects. Thus the sympathetic carries a stimulus which contracts blood-vessels, withholds their food supply from the tissues, and checks all the vital activities of the cells. When a cell or organ is called upon, in the interests of the organism as a whole, either in consequence of a local or of a cerebrospinal stimulus, to exercise its specialized function, to work, it of course requires more food, more oxygen, more nutrition. The checking, repressing action of the sympathetic is withdrawn. By what agency? The question is usually dismissed in our physiological textbooks by saying that there is a ' vaso-motor centre ' in the medulla oblongata. Not to enter here into a detailed examination of the numerous facts that might be adduced to show how inconclusive are the grounds upon which that ' explanation ' is founded, it will suffice to mention that those vaso-motor effects take place after the removal not only of the medulla oblongata, but of the greater part of the spinal cord ; and that further, although vaso-constricting effects result from stimulation of the medulla and of the lateral columns of the cord, no vaso-dilator effect can be observed from their action. After complete removal of the sympathetic from the neck, the ear of a rabbit will regain after a time its normal vascular condition. More, rhythmical vaso-motor phenomena may be observed in small and entirely detached portions of a bat's wing in which artificial circulation is maintained.

The only interpretation that can consistently be placed upon the facts—and it affords the key to the whole mechanism of organic coordination—is that local dilatation of the blood-vessels, increase in the supplies where they are needed, is the effect of the activity of the cells themselves in that part, which *take* more of the common share of supplies when, in the interests of the organism, they need more. The vaso-dilatation is brought about, not by any centre, but by the tissues themselves. And it follows that the checking, ' controlling,' action of the sympathetic, which holds back supplies, is not the effect of the dominance of any ' vaso-motor centre,' but the summation of the needs of all the other elements of the organism. In fine, it is by the equilibrium of the conative impulses of all the elements of the organism maintained at a common resultant level by their organic continuity that the synthetic coordination of the whole is brought about and maintained.

The function of the central nervous system, it is sufficiently clear, is the coordination of the behaviour of the organism as a whole in relation to the external world. Primarily the brain is the organ of coordination of molar movements ; it is a part of the skeletal muscular system. That—not any consciousness—is its primary organic function. Every molar movement of the limbs, wings, body-muscles, is brought about by the combined and finely adjusted action of a large number of muscles. That balanced adjustment necessitates the coordinating action of a distributing centre which shall allot to each muscle the exact amount of stimulation required for its share in the resultant movement. The central nervous system is that coordinating motor centre. Movements which have proved themselves effective by long ancestral experience are permanently combined in fixed connections—reflexes—mostly established in the spinal cord. Movements that are not yet proved and established take place in accordance with the results of cognitive exploration ; and accordingly the organs of sensation must needs be, as they are, arranged in close connection with the motor system of the brain. But it is a quite misleading statement of that fact, and an unwarranted assumption, to say that the brain is the seat of sensation. This is loosely assumed to be proven on the ground of the circumstance that if I cut my median nerve I no longer feel a prick in my finger. I altogether fail to see that the fact that if I cut a telegraph wire the message is not received, is conclusive evidence that no message has been *sent*.

Sensations, however, serve but to guide movements ; they do not originate or determine them. All movement, all behaviour, is the manifestation of dispositions that seek satisfaction through that activity, and make use of sensation to guide them to that consummation. The source of that behaviour is the conative disposition of the organism. And that is neither originated by, or in any way located in, or specially associated with, any brain structure. The brain has nothing to do with the ultimate determinant impulses that give rise to action. It is clear that it is not the brain that is hungry or progenitively disposed, and the tendency to satisfy hunger or love has no particular relation to the brain. The same is true of every conative tendency that is the source of behaviour.

Those conative dispositions are represented in consciousness by the feeling, the affective tone, which is the effect of actual conditions upon them. Those feelings, moods, emotions, have from time immemorial been referred to the various organs of ' vegetative life.' In Hebrew and Oriental literature generally desires and emotions are always located in the bowels—meaning the viscera in general : " The bowels of the wicked are cruel," " Remember, O Lord, thy bowels and kindnesses " ; even the moral impulse and sense of duty was referred to the viscera : " Thy law is in the midst of my bowels." Plato placed courage in the chest and self-regard in the belly. The doctine of ' temperaments ' embodies the same conception in its description of the lymphatic, sanguine, biliary dispositions. Anger and ill-humour are currently ascribed to the liver, envy to the spleen ; though the physicians of Salerno regarded that viscus as the seat of joy, and ascribed love to the liver. Apart from those fancies there are more substantial popular impressions. The state of the mind is commonly observed to depend upon that of the health, of the physiological activities of the body. Much is admitted to depend upon nutrition ; men seek the favour of princes after these have dined ; good assimilation and circulation favour an optimistic outlook, and Carlyle's criticisms of contemporary ideals are usually disposed of by a reference to the condition of his peptic glands.

The manifest correlation between general bodily states, visceral conditions and the affective and conative disposition of the organism are too obvious not to have been taken into account by scientific inquirers. Cabanis expressed the opinion that emotions are dependent upon visceral conditions ; Bichat, with considerable fulness of analysis, laid stress upon the view that " all that relates to the passions pertains to organic life," meaning thereby the life of the visceral organs. It is, however, only comparatively lately that accurate physiological investigation, overcoming the obsession of the doctrine that the brain, and the brain alone, is the ' seat of mind,' has revealed the previously undreamt-of extent and far-reaching magnitude of that correlation. As a result of such studies as those of Mosso, Tanzi, Broca, Lombard, Pawlow, and innumerable other investigators, it is now known that there is not a function or organ, or minutest portion of the organism, which does not register, like the most delicate indicator, the slightest change in the affective state of consciousness. Mental changes so slight as to be quite uninferable from any gross motor expression, and insignificant even in the consciousness of the subject, are represented by definite changes in remote organs and functions. Down to the tips of the fingers and toes, vascular changes, measurable alterations in volume and weight, are associated with the most imperceptible fluctuation of the emotional state. The activity of every gland and the chemical composition of every secretion in the body are affected. The respiratory rhythm soars and sinks, the pupil opens and contracts, the acuteness of the senses undergoes variations in a definite relation to every change in the mental state. There is not a cell or a biochemical reaction of the body that cannot serve as a window through which we may peer into the soul ; so that, as one German physiologist, Born, enthusiastically puts it, " *Die Blase ist der Spiegel der Seele !* " The familiar fundamental proposition of psycho-physiology, ' To every change in the mind there corresponds a change in the brain,' must in view of present knowledge be modified thus : ' To every change in the mind there corresponds a change in every living cell of the organism.'

It is the consideration of such facts—so utterly at variance with the dogma that 'the brain is the organ of mind '—which has suggested the well-known James-Lange ' theory of the emotions,' namely, that an emotional state consists in the sum of the sensations that accompany those organic changes, that it is the disturbed action of the heart and respiration, the pallor, the flushing, the tremors, the dryness of the mouth, the catching at the throat, the perspiration, the ' goose-skin,' which *constitute* an emotional state. Put thus by Lange—who, however, repudiated it later—and by William James, the theory is a psychological ' howler.' For it confounds utterly the primary distinction between the two forms of feeling, the presentative and the affective, sensation and pure feeling. The ' sensations ' referred to are, it is true, those primitive, vague, undifferentiated, quasi-affective cœnaesthesias which are on the borderland of the differentiation. But, on the other hand, the ' emotions' considered in the theory include the most pronounced abstract and sublimated forms of affection associated with the highest developments of presentative consciousness. It is excusable to confound a straight-out ' physical ' pain with a sensation ; that is the primitive level at which cognitive and affective functions are still undifferentiated ; a ' physical' pain may be used either in its cognitive or its affective capacity. But the ' emotion ' produced by grief, by anxiety, by artistic enjoyment, stands at the opposite extreme of the affective scale, and is wholly distinct from any sensory element or function. A man who is overcome by a great sorrow that robs life of its value for him, who is embittered by disappointment, changes the whole course of his conduct, seeks solitude, severs himself from the society of his friends, buries himself in work and thought. His whole conduct is deeply modified, but it is not by the sensation of bitterness in his mouth, of dryness in his throat, or of cold in his feet that it is modified. Sensations are here by-products of the condition ; they are not the determinants, the modifying factors of conduct. Those 'sensations,' moreover, represent only a few of the grosser, more conspicuous of the organic modifications which are the concomitants of affective states ; they are those which we notice without the aid of any physiological investigation. But those are but an infinitesimally small portion of the similar phenomena which accompany emotion ; and of the vast majority of those we are not in the least degree aware, certainly not in the form of sensations. You notice the quickening of your heart and the catching of your breath, but not the increased blood-pressure in your little toe, not the changes in chemical composition in your thyroid gland or your kidneys. To those changes no 'sensation' whatever corresponds. If the few notice-able changes " are the emotion," what are the thousands and thousands of physiological changes that are *not* noticed ?

What is popularly called an 'emotion,' and what is so designated in the Jamesian paradox, is also an abnor-mally pronounced, accentuated, intensified affective state, which forces itself upon our notice by its intensity—what was once upon a time called a 'passion.' That is but a superlative degree of the affective tone which is part of *every* state, however peacefully composed, which is its foundation, which is never absent, and it is the determinant of all modifications of action—external action or secret thought. What applies to an 'emotion' applies equally to the unanalysed, unnoticed affective state of every moment ; if the former be a bundle of sensations, so must the latter be. But that would be to abolish every distinction between feeling and sensation, between affection and presentation ; that is to say, the logical issue of James's theory is exactly what James himself [1] has called 'the psychologist's fallacy.'

[1] *Principles of Psychology*, vol. i, p. 196.

The significance of the physiological law that every cell in the organism is modified with every change in the affective state, becomes at once evident when the nature of the latter is apprehended as the mould in consciousness of the impulses which actuate us, their condition of satisfaction or dissatisfaction. The physiological source of those impulses and conative tendencies, and of our activities, motor or psychical, our acts and our thoughts, our desires and our appetences, is not the brain, but the entire organism, and every living cell that constitutes it. In a somewhat different sense from Aristotle's, the whole of the soul is present in every part of the organism.

The part played by the brain is but one factor in the process ; it does not, in any greater degree than any other portion of the organism, create impulses to action, desires, feelings. Its function is but that of a central junction where the impulses of the organism are brought into relation with the motor organs of external movement, and with the cognitive and sensory organs. Our actions and our thoughts are the resultant of that conjunction. Those elements in the process which constitute our consciousness are not the source, but only modifying factors, of our acts and thoughts. Great as is the importance of the modification which they may bring about, they can only operate upon the material of action which is supplied from other sources, upon impulses which arise from the whole organism. The brain and its conscious processes can do nothing towards creating that material, or determine its ultimate tendencies and direction. The activity of the brain itself, its cognitive processes and its associations, are themselves actuated by impulses which are derived from every part of the organism. It is an organ, an instrument, like all other organs, of the conative forces of the living organism ; a skilled and expert servant, but a servant only of those forces.

With some of the processes taking place in the brain consciousness, we say, is associated. That, we consider, is but the statement of plain and indisputable fact. But, however guardedly that statement may be worded—as by saying that consciousness is ' associated with,' and not that it is ' produced ' or ' generated ' by, the brain—our fundamental and immemorial preconceptions do nevertheless insinuate themselves even in our most punctiliously cautious and uncommitting wording. For in saying that ' consciousness ' exists in relation to those brain-processes, it is assumed and implied that it exists nowhere else, and is not ' associated ' with any other process of the organism, but only with those particular processes of some brain structures. And, whatever views we may profess or repudiate, that bare statement of fact—as we conceive it to be—is tantamount to any of the statements of Victorian materialism, that consciousness is ' produced ' or ' secreted ' by, or is ' a function of the brain ' ; and we are left, in spite of all efforts, irretrievably entangled in all the incongruities and antinomies of ' the relation between mind and matter.'

The actual known fact is in reality slightly different. It is not that ' consciousness ' in general is ' associated ' with the brain, but that what we call ' *our* ' consciousness, that is to say, just that particular sphere of feelings of which we say ' *we* ' are aware, is ' associated ' with those cerebral functions. The bare statement of assured fact does not refer at all to the distribution of ' consciousness,' about which we have no sort of direct knowledge whatever, but to a particular ' field of consciousness.'

That field of consciousness, like the field of vision, has, and can never have more than, one single point of focal distinctness, whence it fades marginally, by a rapid gradation, into blurred indistinctness, faint, and yet fainter awareness. The similarity of the field of consciousness to that of vision is probably not fortuitous ; the disposition of the latter is, doubtless, connected with psychological rather than optical conditions. That structure is a fundamental fact of consciousness. The supposed unextended substance, mind, deliquesces and evaporates at the edges.

The organism at any moment is not affected by *one* interest alone, but is urged and engaged by a countless multitude of coexistent impulses. But those impulses affect it and engage it in greatly varying degrees. Hence there is always among those countless objects of interest one which is foremost, which exceeds all others in the intensity and urgency of its affective value, and is for the instant dominant. That is the focal point of consciousness at the moment.

This is usually expressed by saying that the ' attention ' is directed to that object. The word ' attention ' is almost a superfluous word in psychology, and it is certainly a nuisance and a source of confusion. It is a surviving vestige of a ' faculty of attention ' for which we have no further use. ' Attention,' far from being a faculty, is an act, a reaction, and should be a verbal noun ; it should properly not be ' attention,' but ' attending.'

Attention is of two widely different kinds, corresponding to two distinct types which characterize all our mental operations, acts, thoughts : the directed and the spontaneous type. If a bomb suddenly explodes within twenty yards of you, you will ' pay attention ' to it. Your self-preservative impulses are at once put on the alert and are directed in a lively manner to the object. Food if you are hungry, water if you are thirsty, attract your ' attention,' acquire, that is, a preponderant affective value, an interest beyond all other objects, become the centre, the focus of consciousness. If on opening a book, or your morning paper, you catch sight of an article on a subject in which you are deeply interested, you will read it with avidity, your ' attention ' will be sharply focused on the subject. That is spontaneous attention ; it is the natural operation of your impulses. Your ' attention ' in such cases does not require to be ' directed ' to a given presentation. Your impulse directs itself to the object which most intimately concerns it, and the focus of consciousness is thereby determined.

You may, on the other hand, be performing a task which you have set yourself as a means to some end ; the task itself may be pure drudgery, may be extremely tedious and uninteresting. Your impulses are not in the least implicated in the object directly in hand ; you are going through the task as a matter of lamentable necessity. In order to do it at all it is necessary that each step should in turn become the focal point of your consciousness ; your ' attention ' must be held to the task, artificially directed to its objects ; and other impulses, other presentations which hover in the marginal field, are almost equal in intensity to the artificially maintained focus ; and the narrow margin of preponderance of the latter may at any moment be overstepped, the spontaneous interest violently confined in the marginal area may rise to greater intensity than the artificial focus, which then becomes marginal while the spontaneous interest becomes focal. The attention is distracted. Into the mode of operation of that artificial direction of attention—identical with the controlled direction of thought, of action—we shall not inquire for the present.

That focal consciousness, then, with its narrow field of marginal consciousness, is what we call *our* consciousness. It is our consciousness because it is focal and perifocal, it is focal because it is the prepotent reaction between the dominant conative impulse of our organism at the moment and the object that derives its affective value from its relation to that impulse. Now that position is clearly a relative one. The psychic reaction which occupies the focus of consciousness is but one of a multitude of reactions that are simultaneously taking place between the various conative dispositions of our organism and ambient conditions. It differs from those other psychic reactions solely in the circumstance that it has a higher (spontaneous or artificial) affective value. That intensity is purely relative.

The absolute intensity of the focal consciousness varies within wide limits. The sudden and unexpected menace to our self-preservative instincts, as by the bomb, has an intense value. The mental absorption of the thinker, of Archimedes at the siege of Syracuse incognizant of the invading Roman and of the sword held over his head, is of high intensity. And in proportion as the degree of that intensity exceeds that of concomitant processes these are excluded from the field of consciousness. But from that high intensity the focal consciousness may drop to the most feeble, languid, and blurred condition of dreamy faintness. You may have ' nothing to think of,' you may be bored to apathy, your focal consciousness may idly flutter about and busy itself for want of better to do with the dancing mote or scudding cloud. The focal consciousness at any moment may be by many degrees less intense than the contents of marginal consciousness at another time. The difference between the focal reaction and all others is, then, purely relative, positional. In all other respects, apart from that relative, positional value, those psychic processes, the focal reaction and the marginal ones, are identical in their nature and operation. A psychic process is not rendered less intense because another process happens to be of higher intensity, any more than a building is made smaller by building a higher one alongside.

What constitutes the limelight of focal consciousness is the dominant impulse or interest of the *actual* (i.e. active) moment, the matter in hand ; all psychism, as part of the mechanism of action, being primarily concerned with that. The ' limelight ' is turned upon those mental processes which bear upon the actual matter in hand, which are relevant, and it ignores and excludes all others. The operation of that maximal impulse which determines the focus of consciousness is thus selective.

That selection, that illumination, does not bring those processes into existence or annihilate them, any more than the sweep of a searchlight creates or annihilates the objects which it illumines or leaves in darkness. Those processes which are left in darkness, as not being required in the reaction of the actual moment, do nevertheless continue to take place in relation to impulses which, although in abeyance so far as present action is concerned, are nevertheless operative. The rehearsal of an important action which you are to perform to-morrow occupies your mind, albeit some ' business in hand ' compels you to attend for the moment to quite other things ; the care which you have ' dismissed from your mind ' continues nevertheless to wear you down. While you are reading this page and your consciousness is—we will suppose for the sake of argument—focused on my words, a thousand and one objects of consciousness hover about that focus. You are at the same time raising objections, and passing judgments ; you are thinking of other views which you have read. And at the same time you are ' conscious ' of the weight of the book—the physical weight, I mean—of the chair you are sitting on, of the light you are reading by, of the passing bus, etc., etc. That appointment which you have to keep, and which you might forget while idling your time away over a book of psychology—all those things and a hundred more are hovering on the outskirts of your focal consciousness, so close that the merest trifle will suffice to make them focal and to cause you to fling your book aside.

It is both a logical consequence of the constitution of the field of consciousness, and a matter of common experience, that mental processes of exactly the same kind as those which occupy its focus take place even beyond the indefinite and vaporous edge of its extreme circumference, beyond consciousness. The name that you had forgotten, the problem that you had dismissed from your mind, presently turn up recollected and solved by psychic operations which have not occupied the field of consciousness. You are surprised to find entering into the train of your thoughts some word, some piece of information which you have read or learnt 'without knowing it.'

In a sense well may those trivially familiar phenomena seem surprising and upsetting, for they deal a deathblow to all traditional misconceptions of mind, to the conception that consciousness (i.e. focal and perifocal consciousness) constitutes mind, that separate and distinct entity and substance isolated from all else by impassable gulfs. ' Unconscious mind ' is necessarily, to every conception of traditional psychology, not only a highly questionable, but a wholly inadmissible expression ; one against which academic psychology has felt compelled to lodge an emphatic protest.

But there are grounds more valid than the inviolability of traditional definitions for declining to admit that processes exactly similar to those which take place in focal consciousness can take place apart from consciousness, as, to use Mill's phrase, ' unconscious cerebrations.' For if that were so we should at once be compelled to regard all consciousness as superfluous, as an ' epiphenomenon ' having no part whatever in the functions which it appears to exercise. Such a view is untenable ; for it not only would stultify all knowledge, but it would constitute a unique breach of the most fundamental law of living organization—that no activity can develop that does not serve the conative tendencies of living organisms. If feelings could take place apart from consciousness, there would be no alternative but to adopt the view that they are mere shadows without use or significance. But there is an alternative, the only one, apart from denying the facts or calling them a ' mystery '—and it is to recognize that focal and perifocal consciousness do not constitute the whole of consciousness, and that the circumstance that a psychic operation does not take place within that 'field of consciousness' is no legitimate criterion that it is not accompanied by consciousness.

And it is to that conclusion that the facts themselves point. If it be admitted that each of the ten billion protozoan cells which constitute the human organism reacts individually to the stimuli, internal and external, that affect it, then that reaction is, like all the reactions of life, guided by feeling. The effect of light of the rod- and cone-cells of the retina is not a purely physical effect ; the effect of the pressure of a needle-point on the cells of the cutis is not a purely physical effect. Neither the gratuitous supposition that those impressions are transformed into feeling in the brain alone, nor the very questionable doctrine of specific energies, alters the fact that the reaction of living cells, whether free or forming a part of a metazoic organism, is not an inorganic phenomenon, but postulates those adaptive modifications which are the correlative of feeling. The feelings of the various parts of the organism are only represented in central consciousness as sensations when they are of use in guiding the external motor activities ; where they cannot be thus utilized they are not represented as sensations. The viscera transmit no sensations to the central consciousness ; visceral pain is not the direct effect of the irritant, but of the contractions of the tissues in their efforts to expel it. It is not as sensation, but in the general affective tone of central consciousness which determines the character of the reaction of the organism as a whole, that organic feeling is there represented. Presentative and cogitative processes are not attributable to cell elements severally, for those processes require the combined operation of a vast number of such elements specialized in varied motor and sensory directions ; but if thought were possible to the cells of the liver or the pancreas we should know nothing of it, since it would not be represented in focal consciousness except as a determining affective value. In the brain countless psychic reactions are proceeding simultaneously ; and of those processes only one can be focal. But that focal consciousness, which we call ' our ' consciousness is but one particular perspective, one particular point of view determined by the situation of the actual moment— ' actual ' in the strictest sense, that is, concerned with the action, the reaction of the moment to external circumstances. That consciousness is but an infinitesimal fraction of the totality of psychic processes which take place in preparation for action, and which are actuated by every impulse manifesting itself in the organism. ' Our ' consciousness is an aspect of the psychic activity of every living element of our organism ; but it is not the whole of that activity.

The brain, and its amœboid cells with their pseudopods and tentacles, are not the seat of some unique and mysterious power or principle, of a miraculous function to be found there alone. Their function, however portentous its results, does not involve any new activity, but only the coordinated operation of activities and powers which are inherent in all living substance. The affective tone, the degree of satisfaction or dissatisfaction of the conative dispositions which actuate all systems of living energy, can, we have seen, be differentiated and specialized into cognitive feeling. Affective tones, however complex, are reproduced in the reaction of any living system to a situation or symbolic perception corresponding to that affective value. That reproduction projects itself into all the motor and sensory groups of elements that are associated with the activity towards which that state tends ; or, vice versa, any sensori-motor complex, such as is called up by a word (the associated sound-symbol of that complex) will reproduce the affective values of that symbol, thus forming them into a concept. Every concept is in ultimate analysis a complex of sensory and motor presentations, and its physiological counterpart is the activity of the cortical and thalamic cell-groups which would receive the various sensations and correlate the various movements which make up that concept. Cognitive conation, urged by the interests of the moment, can juxtapose any number of concepts, and in turn perceive their likeness or unlikeness in respect to values determined by the actuating interest, as the protozoon distinguishes the likeness or unlikeness of two affective states.

It is as a resultant of primary activities that the age-long elaborated experience of cognitive and motor acts has been moulded into the instrument of the conative tendencies inherent in all life, a functional and intermittent and precarious resultant interrupted by states of unconsciousness.

There are several ' theories of sleep ' which serve to display the obscurity in which our conceptions of the fundamental principles of vital reaction are still enwrapt. The blood-supply of the brain can be shown to be increased during the activity and reduced during the resting-time of central consciousness ; and accordingly the theory has been put forth that anæmia of the brain is the cause of sleep. But the facts of blood circulation and pressure are the same for every organ of the body ; each obtains a larger blood-supply when it is active than when it is inactive. To say that anæmia of the brain is the cause of sleep is much as if we should say that congestion of the brain is the cause of thought, or that increased blood-supply to my muscles is the cause of my playing a game of tennis, and anæmia of those muscles the cause of my sitting down.

Others offer as an explanation of sleep the partial intoxication or clogging of nerve-cells by their own waste-products or by the acid waste-products thrown into the circulation by the general activities of the body (Preyer, Obersteiner), or the exhaustion of intracellular oxygen (Pflüger). Those again are not phenomena that are peculiar to nerve-cells, they are common to all tissues. The nerve-cells of the ganglia of bees and of sparrows have been studied after the day's exertion and after the night's repose, and have been found to become shrivelled and loaded with the accumulations of fatigue-stuffs. That is as one would expect. But Claparède, on the other hand, has pointed out with considerable elaboration that animals and men settle down to sleep at given hours, whether they are in a state of exhaustion or no, and that going to sleep at certain intervals is a matter of habit, of instinct, the utility of which is clearly to forestall actual exhaustion. That view, which is manifestly in accordance with facts, shows that we are to regard sleep not as an effect of exhaustion but as an *act* designed to guard against it ; but it does not tell us how that act is performed.

The only theory that does attempt to supply such an explanation is that put forward by the great Spanish histologist, Ramón y Cajal. According to his view, supported by Duval, Waldeyer, Lépine, Lugaro, and others, the dendritic fibrils of the cells of the cortex retract during sleep sufficiently to break off their physiological connection with other cells, and it is to that break in the connection that the loss of central consciousness is due.

Here we have a real explanation. The only objection that has been offered against it is that it is not proved. It is a matter of very considerable difficulty to render visible by the most elaborate methods of staining the minute arborizations of the delicate, translucent pseudopods of dead nerve-cells ; it is, of course, out of the question to observe living ones, in the higher animals at least. Yet Waldeyer has actually succeeded in observing living nerve-cells in a transparent crustacean, *Leptodera hyalina*, and found the pseudopodial processes of those cells to be as active during life as those of a rhizopod. Under artificial stimulation those amœboid movements have been observed by Rüchardt, Duval, and Kölliker. No other view appears plausible than that the neurons of the brain, those protozoa of thought, effect the connections and concatenations upon which motor and cognitive coordination depend by the movements of their pseudopods; and it appears inconceivable that those delicate protoplasmic tentacles thrust in all directions, identical in the minutest detail of their structure with the lace-like pseudopods of a radiolarian, are in the living state motionless and rigid structures such as we see them silver-stained in the paralysis of death.[1]

Cajal and Duval assume that in sleep it is the connection between the terminal arborizations of the afferent sense elements and the recipient cells of the cortex and thalamus, that is dissevered, so as to

[1] That the functional connection between one nerve-cell, or *neuron*, and another is effected by the pseudopodial movements of the cells themselves is further evidenced by the following facts :— Electrical stimulation of a nerve-fibre, that is, of the axis-cylinder process of a neuron, is conducted equally well in both directions, whether the cell have an afferent or efferent function. But if a nerve-path including *two* spinal neurons, and where an interneuronic junction is therefore interposed, be stimulated, conduction will only take place in *one* direction ; the arborizations of the extremity of the axis-cylinder of one cell being stimulated to effect a connection with the body of the other cell, while the latter, not possessing any arborizations in that direction, is unable to effect a connection with the extremity of the axis-cylinder of the other cell. Where, however, the arrangement is different, and both cells possess dendritic processes at the same junction, as in the nerve-cells of Medusa, the stimulus is propagated equally well in *both* directions.

Stoppage of the circulation, and the application of various poisons only affect very slowly the conductivity of the nerve-trunk of a cell to stimuli, but it almost at once abolishes the transmission of a stimulus from one cell to another.

The latent period of reaction, that is, the time that elapses between the application of a stimulus and its end effect, is greatly increased by the presence of an interneuronic junction in the path of conduction ; and that delay is proportional to the number of such neuronic junctions.

That the stimulus of functional activity is necessary in order that nerve-cells should put out dendritic processes at all has been shown by Berger, who examined the cells of the visual centres of young dogs, some of which had been blinded from birth. While the visual neurons of the normal dogs showed the usual complex pseudopodial arborizations, those of the blind animals had remained embryonic and showed no trace of any pseudopodial processes.

exclude sensory impressions. It appears, however, more probable that it is between the higher cortical centres of coordination and those below them, which are actuated by the afferent somatic impulses of the organism at large, that the break is to be sought. Insomnia is of two types, the one connected with intense intellectual or sensory excitement, where the higher coordinating centres of the cortex and the sensory centres are highly stimulated ; the other with intense emotional states, grief, worry, joy, and every form of affective excitement. In the one it is the activity of the intellectual centres which prevents the disconnection, in the other it is that of the afferent affective paths. In those conditions sleep may be induced by fixing consciousness on an object of no interest, an indifferent thought, or by monotonous (but not by emotionally expressive) sounds, so as to exclude intellectual and emotional interests from the focus of consciousness. Similarly, artificial hypnosis is brought about by fixing the attention on an object devoid of interest or significance, such as a bright point and thus endeavouring, as in going to sleep, to ' think of nothing at all.'

In dreams conscious operations are ' undirected,' they are withdrawn from the coordinative influence of the intellectual centres, from all habitual paths of word-thought, of convention, in which it dwells during waking life ; and the deeper conative impulses of the organism, uninfluenced by the higher centres, have free play.

Similarly is the grip and dominance of the cognitive cells relaxed in alcoholic intoxication ; the shackles of routine and convention are loosened and the impulsive forces which they smothered are set free. Under the Dionysian inspiration man becomes himself and shamelessly begins to utter truth and be fearless. The natural conative forces and living desires assume command of their cognitive instruments of symbolic thought and become creative, and the liberated man feels as if a god spoke within him. Till presently the drugged organs are further weakened ; the forces whose high developments arose in relation to them, the higher avatars of the conative impulses, are left without instruments ; only the lower remain. The god sinks into the brute. The retracted pseudopods of the bedoped cortical cells further shrivel and shrink, and the beast sinks helpless to sleep off his brief madness.

The deeper causation of our psychic life, the springs of our activities, of our desires and motives, of our moods and character, do not lie in the superficial realm of perceptions and ' associations of ideas,' in that limited realm of focal consciousness which was wont to constitute ' the soul,' and was placidly introspected by scholastic psychology as an isolated and self-contained microcosm. Mental causation, the connection between one idea and another, between one affective state and another, between the various determinants and factors of behaviour, the causes of our acts and thoughts, are not to be found in that narrow realm. There are quite other causes than the ' motives ' and ' purposes ' of which we are aware, than the perceptible connections discoverable by introspection. Of much more consequence in those processes are physiological and biological laws and events which are as yet entirely obscure to us. As, for instance, the various protean transformations of the reproductive impulse ; the rhythms and periodicities in all vital activities, of which the individual life, its cycle of youth, maturity, age, and death, with their transformations, is itself one. There is—to mention but an instance— besides the daily cycle through which all our powers and dispositions ebb and flow, a monthly periodicity which was probably established when our ancestors lived in an ambient of tidal waters, and which, far from being confined to one particular manifestation in woman, is of the first importance in the physiological and psychological state of both sexes. The determination and issue of our mental activities and behaviour is essentially connected with such facts, and a thousand more which our physiology and biology are scarcely even ready to approach.

Nor is that all. The character of the dispositions and activities of our organism is of necessity affected by every physical agency that acts upon it, quite independently of any perception or knowledge we may have of that action. Atmospheric conditions, temperature, pressure, moisture, electrical states and disturbances, have their deep-working and inevitable influence upon all the functions and reactions of our organism, and many of us are well aware of the effect of those conditions upon their functions and moods. The total disposition of our organism, the source and determination of our feelings and of our acts, are thereby modified. There is not, to be quite consistent, an event in the universe which has not its ineludible repercussion in the physical state of our organism, and therefore in the constitution of our mind ; the sun, moon, and planets inevitably exercise upon every molecule and atom of our bodies, and consequently upon the inmost springs of our soul, an influence more ineludible than any ever dreamed of by astrological fancy. The causation of our acts and of our thoughts includes the entire universe.

CHAPTER VII

CONTROL AND FREEDOM

THE unity of a highly complex and differentiated living organism, manifested in the minute precision of the adjustments which coordinate the manifold activities of its parts, becomes intelligible in the light of that fundamental principle which I have described in the foregoing chapter as the Law of Equilibrium. We have now to consider certain consequences of that law which give rise to results of a seemingly opposite kind. How, for instance, if the conative dispositions actuating every reaction of the organism are identical throughout every part of it, can such a thing as a 'conflict of motives' take place at all? Such a conflict within an organism which is marked by the perfection of the self-adjustment of every one of its activities to all others, is a fact which ought indeed on any view to appear somewhat surprising. Again, in accordance with that principle, we regarded the activities of the central consciousness as fundamentally determined, like all other functions, by the conative disposition common at any moment to all parts of the organism—a view which led us to emphasize what in the traditional language of dualism is spoken of as 'the influence of the body on the mind.' But, while that aspect is universally admitted, the converse aspect, 'the influence of the mind on the body,' is no less manifest. So much so that the central consciousness, hypostatized into a distinct entity, 'the mind,' 'the soul,' has immemorially been conceived as 'ruling' the body or 'earthly

tenement ' in which it dwelt, using it for *its* purposes,
pulling, as it were, its various levers and springs, and
operating its various organs or instruments on its own
behalf. That primitive scheme, whatever modifications it
may in later times have undergone, still substantially
represents the vague current conceptions of psycho-
physiological organization. And, not only does it represent
the popular notion ; its influence can be traced in the
most fundamental principles of our scientific physiology,
however ' materialistic ' its professors. For ' the soul '
substitute the brain, and our most advanced physiological
science reproduces the antique Oriental picture of a
ruler who from his exalted seat imposes his will upon
the drilled and obedient multitude of his servants, sending
hither and thither orders and messages, ' nervous impulses,'
which direct and control, ' stimuli ' which set organs
working, ' inhibitions ' which veto their activity. Under
the hegemony of that supreme ruler are hosts of minor
potentates, ' controlling centres,' which in their own sphere
repeat the same autocratic rule—' control,' ' stimulate
and ' inhibit.'

Whatever the grounds that originally gave rise to those
conceptions, and the fantastic forms which they have
at times assumed, it would be idle to pretend that ample
colour is not lent to them by facts which are quite manifest
and most naturally lend themselves to that interpretation.
The central consciousness does appear to exercise a unique
controlling influence upon the bulk of the activities of
the organism.

There is, however, no contradiction between those
facts and the law of equilibrium. The reactions arising
out of the conative dispositions common to all organs
and functions differ according as the varied ambient
conditions of each part and the differentiated functions
which it discharges are different. In the vast majority
of cases no differentiation in specialized activity can give
rise to any conflict between one function and another,

or to the dominance of one organ over others ; for the actuating impulse is the same in all. What is the ' interest,' the feeling, of one is likewise that of all other organic elements ; and every mutual adjustment takes place by virtue of that equalized level of the sources of action, and of the feelings that represent them, throughout all the constituent parts of the organism. Conflict and dominating precedence can, however, arise in respect of one function, and one function only, that, namely, of cognition.

So long as an organism is actuated by pure impulses alone and its consciousness is limited to pure feeling, there can be no conflict of motives, no hesitation or choice in its behaviour. The operation of two impulses tending in opposite directions, such as a self-preservative and a reproductive impulse, does not give rise to a conflict, but to an automatic resultant depending upon their respective strength in the circumstances of the moment. The organism is an automaton. But every *cognitive* act implies, as we have seen, a ' conflict of motives.' A cognition is the substitution for the feeling of the moment— the primitive determinant of action—of the presentation of a prospective feeling which is not actually present, but is impending in the future, of a hope or a fear for an actual pleasure or pain. Cognition is a fundamental modification of feeling, as feeling is a modification of conation. But, apart from that inherent conflict between a presented and an actual feeling, which attaches to all cognition, it follows from the function of any element cognitively differentiated that it exercises, by virtue of that function, an authority over other elements. No cognition can be transmitted organically as such. An element or organ that fulfils that function does not, and cannot, transmit ' information,' cognition, to other organs. Only the conative tendency, the feeling that represents it, can be transferred and distributed by way of organic continuity. The organism is accordingly dependent upon its cognitive elements; it must 'take their word,' so to speak, rely on them, and conform in its attitude and behaviour towards changes in its external relations to their report. To determine these conditions and therefore the attitude of the whole organism towards them, is precisely the function of cognitive activities. Those activities are actuated by conations common to the whole organism, but the modification of behaviour brought about by the cognitive reaction is determined by the organ of cognition. Hence inevitably a privileged supremacy of all cognitive elements.

In the cells around the mouth of the primitive metazoon the efforts of the organism to discriminate and explore the environment and the future are centred; and in that region all cognitive specialization will take place: the body will be led by the head. With the extension of the range of forestalling cognition and of the scope of means, and the consequent multiplication of instrumental purposes and possible action, that dependence is correspondingly increased; and so is at the same time the contrast and conflict between the far-ranging presentations of cognition and the actual feeling of the moment.

The neuro-muscular apparatus which comprises the central nervous system and the sense-organs together with the limbs and skeletal muscles, constitutes in the vertebrates a single, structurally correlated organ of external behaviour. The parts of that system operate, as regards their specialized activity, not directly through the equilibrium of the conative impulses of the organism, but mediately through the motor cells of the brain, as a single structural system. The dependence of that apparatus upon the brain is quite different from the dependence of the visceral organs on the brain. The operation by which I move my arm, and that by which my gastric glands are set secreting at the sight of food are physiologically two utterly different operations. The idea of a given movement can in the one case give rise to that movement, for the 'idea' is itself the activity of the very cells in the motor areas of the brain which produce it. Brain and muscular apparatus are a ready-assembled machine whereby desire is transformed into movement. And within that machine itself the conception of a controlling brain is so far accurate. But the brain cannot send 'orders' to organs outside the neuro-muscular apparatus; there is no provision whereby the brain can determine the secretion of the gastric glands. These are stimulated, like the muscle of the arm, by the 'idea' of food; but what is transmitted to them by the brain is what it transmits to every portion of the organism, the affective change which that perception or that presentation brings about. It is the equilibration of the affective state of the whole organism, to which the gastric glands react. Though both activities follow upon an 'idea,' the one is said to be 'voluntary' and the other not.

It is the disproportionate development of the functions of cognition and molar movement in higher organisms that gives rise to the semblance of a supreme authority; but that authority is in reality exercised within the special sphere only of one apparatus, which is itself but the instrument of the conations of the whole organism.

That sphere of cognitive instrumentality has assumed in the 'human faculty' proportions so colossal that they constitute a seemingly 'separate world,' in which the focal consciousness has come to dwell almost exclusively. Between that new world of cognition and the rest of the organism an ever widening cleft has been opened. Intellect is hopelessly isolated from the organism by a linguistic barrier, it speaks a different tongue; it cannot transmit thoughts, concepts, judgments, words to the organism which only understands the language of affections, of feeling, of emotion. A solitude is spread around the intellectual consciousness, the loneliness of the thinker.

Thus has come about in actual fact a separation, a

contrast, an opposition, between the cogitating consciousness and ' the body.' The latter has become ' the beast,'
and its spontaneous conative impulses have become ' the
lower impulses.'

The illusion thus created is, of course, an illusion merely.
The enormously hypertrophied functions and organs of
cognition are, for all their abnormal dimensions, but
organs *of* the body. They do not use the body as an
instrument, but, on the contrary, are themselves used as
instruments by the body ; for they are in fact actuated
not by any motive power peculiar to, and inherent in
themselves, but by the conative dispositions of the organism
as a whole. That ' separate world ' of theirs, as it has
come to appear, is nothing but the sphere of ways and
means by which the conative tendencies of the whole
organism, and not of the brain alone, are carried out. It is
to that sphere of *means*, of instrumentality in the operation
of impulses, that the world of conscious action is confined.
The contrast, the dualism, only exists between that vastly
extended sphere of means, and the obscurity, the *unconsciousness*, into which the actuating forces are thus thrust
away by the conscious intellect.

It must not be overlooked, on the other hand, that
those hypertrophied organs of cognition are themselves
a part of the ' organism as a whole ' ; they too have
their share in the determination of the resultant of the
equilibrated conative disposition common to the entire
organism. That dispositon is perpetually modified in the
most momentous manner by the affective changes to
which cognition gives rise. Conation, we have seen, can
only become actualized through the self-revelation of
experiential proof. And it is accordingly by the gigantic
expansion of the field of experience in conceptual consciousness that the conative dispositions of life are set free in
the vastness of a new world to assume the forms of new
appetences, of aspirations which transcend its primitive
organic forms, its physiological and instinctive reactions

fixed in primordial structure and function, and reduce them to the status of ' lower impulses.'

Between those fixed dispositions and the forms of conation developing in the opportunities of larger experience there arise of necessity ' conflicts of motives.' Such conflicts are dependent, it must not be forgotten, upon cognition ; they are not so much conflicts between impulses themselves as between their claim to the present means of operation, or their subordination to the future, to a more remote realization. And it is the expansion of the range of outlook, its protension from the actual moment to eternity itself, which gives rise to the complexity and significance of the conflict. One and the same impulse can quite well give rise to a conflict of motives—the desire, for instance, to have our cake and eat it.

As a matter of fact a conflict of motives only does arise in a situation that is *new*. In situations which are familiar, habitual, nothing of the sort can happen. We react to the familiar situation automatically, because there is nothing in that situation to be cognitively discovered ; cognition is not called upon to operate. And accordingly between the perception of the occasion for their activity and the reaction of our conative impulses there intervenes no conflict, no deliberation, no conscious psychological process at all. Introspective observation searches in vain in such a reaction of our being for any trace of a process of volition, for any manifestation of ' the will ' ; and we say that our behaviour is reflex, is fixed in instinctive reaction, in custom, in habit. It takes place without any intervention, except in the recognition of the situation, of the processes of cognitive consciousness. It is the straight-out reaction of our established conations to the situation to which they are already adjusted.

It is only when faced with a situation which is novel, or is rendered so by the tampering interference of thought, that any conflict of motives ever does, or ever can, arise. The conative dispositions of the organism are then called upon to adjust themselves to a new situation, to devise a new means of satisfaction, a new mode of reaction. And it is that adjustment, that process of adaptation, which constitutes the conflict of motives. The 'hesitations' of the organism are the oscillations in which the equilibrium disturbed by the new cognitive experience readjusts itself.

The inhibition by an unpleasant experience of an old-established impulse can only be temporary. The unpleasant impression will, after a time, fade, and the established impulse reassert itself. Only through repetition can the modification be established permanently ; and in general the more fundamental impulse—which does not mean the most habitually operative—tends to prevail ; as, for instance, the reproductive over the self-preservative impulse.

The discussion of conflicts of motives has generally been undertaken from the point of view of the moral philosopher, and made an occasion to slop high sentiments over moral values, to the detriment of the scientific attitude. That brilliant and perverse writer, William James, stamps his heels with fiendish glee on all logic and science by proclaiming that the 'will' of the hero 'follows the path of greatest resistance.' Such language is doubtless edifying, but it is neither illuminating nor true. The operation of motives is not a theme of ethics, but of psychology, and all the phenomena of ideo-motor conflict and inhibition are just as clearly exhibited by the villain as by the hero.

There is no 'following the path of greatest resistance' in any conflict of motives. Every one of us yields in every moment of his life present satisfactions to perceived future advantages. The 'sacrifice' is even established as a barely conscious automatic habit in all the drudgery, the beseeming deportment, the conformity of our routine of life. All human behaviour is governed by deterrents and inducements, by hopes and by fears, by the prevalence of prospective values over those of the moment ; and it is the function of all cognitive processes to carry out that substitution. The gold-hunter who faces the troglodytic conditions of life in Alaska in the hope of making a fortune sacrifices the present to the future. And the entire organization of capitalistic society is founded on reliance on the psychological necessity of wage-earners to submit to the utterly distasteful necessity of working, under the pressure of the ideo-motor force of threatening starvation and the inducement of wages. All inhibition of present reluctance is governed by the powerful forces of inducements and deterrents. That relation constitutes nine hundred and ninety-nine parts of the mechanism of human life. We do not what actual, present impulse urges us to do, but what the ideo-motor power of inducements and deterrents determines.

Psychologically every man has his price. Every one is ready to bear present discomfort or pain in view of clearly perceived advantage disproportionate to that discomfort or that pain.

The moral philosopher's opportunity arises when the determining inducement thins out from gross, obvious, crude considerations of future consequences, on the same plane as the values of the present situation, to motives of attenuated abstraction. But there is no essential difference in the psychological mechanism of the martyr's choice and that of the most trivial foresight of daily life.

It is stated as a principle, and repeated in every psychological textbook, that abstract ideas have a more feeble ideo-motor value than concrete ones. Now that is simply not true. Men—not saints or philosophers, but common herds and crowds—are constantly frenzied into fantastic follies, reckless of all else, by abstract ideas. Abstract ideas are, in fact, the only things—except love—that will induce men to lay down their lives. The motive power of ideas, their efficiency as modifiers of action, does not depend upon their being concrete or abstract, but in the degree in which they are *believed*.

Belief is the condition of every idea's power as a determinant of action ; and the degree of that power depends upon the degree of belief. The whole end of cognitive processes is to bring about a degree of belief adequate to warrant action in accordance with it. The supposed feebleness of ' abstract ' ideas as motives has nothing to do with their abstractness, but arises from the circumstance that, in most cases, abstract ideas are not so vividly, so completely believed in as concrete ones. We are extremely prone—in the artificial symbolism of our word-consciousness—to *profess* belief, to believe that we believe in notions which, in reality, we believe in very imperfectly or not at all. The professed belief, the idea which we choose to persuade ourselves to believe that we believe, has, of course, no ideo-motor force at all. The fact of belief consists wholly and solely in its motive power. If we really do believe in a notion, it matters not one jot whether it be abstract or concrete ; of the two the abstract belief will probably be the most intractable determinant of action. To the ignorant martyr, to the Mahdist who rushes the machine-guns at Omdurman, his convictions are an even more powerful inducement than wages to the proletarian workman. And in the days when the latter *believed* in ' duty ' and in religion, he required far less inducement in the form of wages. The ' will ' of the fanatic, the obstinacy of the unthinking, is as the strength of ten because their hearts are pure from doubting thought.

Uncertainty, hesitation, wavering, weakness of the will, are introduced by thinking. The native hue of resolution is sicklied o'er with the pale cast of thought. With intellectualism you have the true dissolution of the will, the hesitancy of action paralysed by unformed and qualified cognition. Your thinker is ousted in the field

of action by the curt decision of the individual of limited
and narrow thought, to whom his formulas are real, and
who looks with the contempt of the man of action upon
the *idéologue*.

But thought, while it is the shatterer of primitive
credulity and primitive resolution, is likewise the true
creator of the highest forms of will. ' Strength of will '
in that higher sense is the product of thought. If the
ideo-motor concept which conflicts with the present
impulse is the final conclusion of a full consideration
that has left no loophole for the *re*consideration of
unforeseen aspects, its power is developed in its full
degree.

The methodological fault of the stereotyped psychological discussion on the ' conflict of motives ' situation
lies in confining consideration chiefly on the hesitating
mind at the moment when it is confronted with the
necessity of choice. It is not in the conflict itself, but
in its antecedents, that the determining action of ' will '
can be rightly appreciated. That ' will ' is a product
of cognitive evolution. The crux of its power lies not in
the conflict of choice, but in the antecedent process of
resolution ; it is the latter that bestows upon an idea
its ideo-motor power. The force of the will depends not
on any ' I will,' but on the thoroughness of our self-
analytic survey. If that has not been complete, if it has
not been sufficiently honest and sincere, a loophole is
still left for ex-tempore decision, and our ' resolution '
stands in danger of being a mere New-Year's resolution
subject to conflicts of motives. The assurance with which
you deal with a situation on principles the bearings of
which you have fully and maturely considered, is identical
with the assurance with which you speak on a subject
on which you possess full and detailed knowledge and which
you have long meditated. The strongest will is the most
deliberate, the longest will. Giordano Bruno, the supreme
historical example of the martyr's choice under the

inspiration of purely abstract ideas, did not make that choice in a moment of exaltation on the theatre of his triumph, but daily and hourly during seven long years of imprisonment in which every inducement was offered to him to admit the expediency of a lie.

The same long-drawn process is exhibited in Plato's account of the resolution of Socrates not to avail himself of Crito's offers of rescue : " All my life, not only now, I have been a man who can obey no friend but reason, the reason that seems best to me after I have thought the matter out. And the reasons I used before I cannot give up now, because this has befallen me. I honoured and reverenced them before ; they seem much the same still. And if we have nothing better to bring forward now, you may be sure I shall not give my consent." [1]

' Strength of will ' consists in having completely ' made up one's mind ' ; there is no other secret about it. All the tasks, the aims, that we contemplate and which we should desire to be sufficiently ' strong ' to achieve, are in reality surprisingly easy of achievement. The one condition required is that all *other* aims, all other tasks, shall be ruthlessly discarded and set aside. Most people, for instance, would very much like to become rich, and they lament that they find it so difficult to make money. Now it is one of the easiest things in the world to make money. It is almost impossible to avoid becoming a millionaire should one undertake the task. The sole condition is that all other aims whatsoever shall be surrendered. And that is precisely what prevents people from becoming rich. Those weak-minded ones desire wealth, but only as a means to other things. They would like to make money and at the same time to enjoy it and spend it. That, of course, is futile. If you wish to make money you must not think of enjoying yourself, of doing this, that or the other ; you must think of nothing else, value no other motive than that of making money.

[1] *Crito,* 46, b, c.

And you will inevitably become a millionaire with wealth beyond the dreams of avarice, and not a notion of how to spend it, not a possibility of any other satisfaction under the sun.

So it is of every aim, of every task. Whether you accomplish it and achieve your purpose does not depend on whether you are endowed with a strong will or afflicted with a weak one. It depends on whether you have once for all clearly and beyond all possibility of repentance estimated the value of the task to you, and decided how much you are prepared to sacrifice to it. You have other desires ; is your purpose of such value to you that you will sacrifice those other desires to its accomplishment ? If you have once clearly judged that it is so, that nothing else, that purpose unaccomplished, will afford you true satisfaction, that you can never repent that satisfaction, that you must always regret the non-satisfaction of the desire that urges you—then, when opposing motives are brought before you, there will no longer be any ' conflict of motives,' none at least the issue of which can be in doubt. You have resolved the conflict beforehand.

The drawback to all such focused volition is the very sacrifice it entails. We can only have one character if that character is to possess any ' strength '; if our character is formed in the only way in which it can be formed, that is, from a single point of view, it is necessarily a horrible character from every other point of view. To be many-sided we must be weak. Focus your character, your aim, your conduct, and you have the squalid destitution of the millionaire, the horrible selfishness of the idealist. That is inevitable.

The old theologico-juridical notion that responsibility depends upon knowledge is wholly justified. No ideomotor abstract can be prepotent over another, can prevail, unless it is clearly known, apprehended, *believed* to be in reality truer, higher, of higher value. In our criminal classes the traditional notions of our morality are, of course, perfectly familiar ; but they are not believed. The professional thief regards all the conventions of property as but legalized theft ; his ' conscience ' holds him perfectly justified, his only deterrent is the police. To a society which is fundamentally immoral, which is founded on principles which no longer inspire belief, which have become transparent lies, it is impossible to enforce its conventional morality. So long as theft, adultery, murder, perjury, are legalized and justified in a society, it is in vain for it to expect a moral stigma to attach to particular forms of theft, of adultery, of perjury, of murder.

The control of thought, the control of ' attention,' consist in exactly the same psychological mechanism as the control of conduct by the determination of an idea, of a principle. In order to carry out any train of thinking, a task must be set to thought. And the ' attention,' the focus of consciousness is held to that set task by the inducement or deterrent power of a consideration which supplies the affective motive that makes the relevant ideas focal, and prevents impulses which are tending to break through the control of that idea from becoming focal. Apart from that ideo-motor control which furnishes a relevant, consistent, ' association ' of ideas, thought is naturally rhapsodic, incoherent. Its ' associations of ideas,' if undirected by the controlling influence of a set task, will not be at all the Hartleyan laws of orderly association, but will be supplied by impulses, secret, maybe, and unavowed, which will use the kaleidoscopic sequence of conscious presentations as symbols of their affective states. Undirected cogitative behaviour is what, but for the control of ideas, be they but the common conventions of civilized deportment, the external behaviour of a person would be who should walk the street and obey every primordial impulse as it arose, until safely locked up.

It is one and the same mechanism that constitutes all noetic psychic action from the dawn of cognition to the highest human conduct—the modification of immediate reaction by the presented anticipation of a future and the reflection of a past ; the influence upon the actual instant of something which appears to exist only as a feeling, an idea, a thought ; the effect of things invisible upon things visible, of mind over matter. That control is the expression of the time-protension of life by its perpetual renewal ; and it is the character of its reactions from the first rudiments of sensation to the human faculty ; it is that protension in time which, looking before and after, stretches out the span of reaction from the present instant to eternity ; it is psychic control, it is free-will.

The sempiternal question of free-will presents itself under three main aspects : the first of these is a misconception, a pseudo-question ; the second involves the very foundations of our logic and world-conception ; the third is a question of scientific fact.

If we put entirely out of consideration physical causation and the extent to which the sequence of mental events is bound up with it, we are left, nevertheless, with a sequence of causation as definite as any which we may recognize in the physical world—and one, indeed, which we have much more valid grounds for recognizing ; for in the physical world we perceive the sequence merely, whereas in consciousness we perceive not only the sequence, but also the nexus in terms of psychological values between one mental state and another. That connection is the more manifest the more our mental processes are controlled by a directing purpose or ideo-motor principle, a cognition.

The fact of that coherent causal sequence is, by a strange confusion, conceived to be in contradiction with the notion of ' freedom.' That notion, and the whole question as to whether we can lay claim to that freedom, does not arise from any abstract idea of freedom, but from a certain undismissible, intuitive sense which we designate by that name. And it is with that sense or persuasion, and not with any abstractly defined ' freedom,' that the causality of mental processes is in the first instance contrasted. And that intuition which protests against every discursive conclusion that would bely it does not at all proclaim the anarchy of consciousness, and claim it to be a delirium of inchoate inconsequence, but, on the contrary, emphatically claims a sensible orderliness, a discreet rule and power of determination. It is not any abstracted theoretical ' freedom ' which our common-sense demands, but the freedom *of the will*. That expression belongs, unfortunately, to a primitive faculty-psychology in terms of which we can no longer think ; but it is perfectly clear that what is meant by it is the *control* which a presentation constituting an inducing hope or deterrent fear exercises over present feeling and conation, the control which an idea exercises over thought and action, the control which a set purpose exercises over the sequence of our thoughts and acts. But that relation is precisely the principle of causation in cognitive consciousness. Our sense and intuition of freedom is the consciousness of the psychological relation between mental facts. We feel that sequence to be governed by the psychological value of the facts just as it appears to us in consciousness ; and that relation constitutes our sense of freedom. In short, the sense of freedom which we have, and which is so vivid that hardly any argument can shake it, arises from that self-same psychological causation which in our theorizing is opposed to it, that is, to itself.

So long, then, as we confine ourselves to those intuitive grounds on the strength of which we claim ' freedom ' for our ideo-motor control, far from there being any sort of opposition between that intuition and mental causation, the two are identical, and the latter constitutes the very ground of our claim.

It is when we pass from that particular case of causation to the principle of causality in general, and from the particular intuition of freedom to the converse principle of necessity in general, that we come upon a dilemma which bears upon the particular question of our mental causation only inasmuch as it bears upon every causation and every event actual or possible.

We only know of such a thing as *necessity* as a logical rule by means of which we operate for cognitive purposes our processes of conceptual thought. Apart from that technical use we know of no such thing in the universe. When the notion is applied to the course of events which we observe to take place uniformly, to the ' laws of nature,' the predication is not only grossly illegitimate, it is wholly inapplicable and essentially unmeaning. Whatever can be deduced by virtue of logical necessity alone, exists already in the data from which it is deduced ; and therefore nothing can ever *happen* by virtue of necessity.

The only ' necessity ' known to us is logical and mathematical necessity. But *that* is only the effect of the groping feebleness of our mental processes, which compels us to deploy and explicate what is all the while contained in our premises and data, and what we might see there directly and immediately without any laborious explication were our mental grasp a little stronger and our vision a little keener. That logical necessity only comes into existence from our intellect's need of a crutch. We demonstrate at length what is implicit in our datum, and thus draw from that a *necessary* consequence, much in the same way as we use paper and pencil to ' work out ' relations which with a little more acuteness and concentration we might ' work out ' without that aid. To demonstrate is merely to point out what is staring us in the face. It requires a laboured demonstration to show that a notion of ours is nonsense because it affirms a thing and denies it in the same breath. But it is not our demonstration *per necessitatem* that makes it nonsense ; it *is* nonsense all along, whether we demonstrate it or no, and whether the ' stupidity against which the very gods fight in vain ' can or cannot perceive the force of our demonstration.

And so likewise when we explicate mathematically the implicit consequences of our data, we are but spelling out what has already been told us in those data. The conclusion to which we arrive at the end of our calculation is not the consequence of our calculation, but of our data— hence it is *necessary*. The *data* of the mathematician always include all the powers involved in the problem, and also their qualities ; for mathematics can only deal with *quantities*, and can therefore never evolve a new source of power or a new quality of power from its data. ' Give me matter and motion, and I will construct the universe,' says the mathematician. Allowing for the naïve conception that ' matter and motion ' are the constituents of the universe, what is meant by that feat is this : ' Give me all the powers of the universe and their qualities, and also the " laws " of operation of those powers, that is, the way in which those powers act ; give me also an initial position or disposition of those powers from which to start—if you give me all those things as data, there being now nothing else in the universe to give, I will proceed to perform the feat of constructing a universe which is already constructed.'

The mathematical physicist's boast is inspired by his knowledge of the *laws* of physical action, which—since he knows them—he omits to mention among his desiderated data. And it is those laws of physical behaviour which he and others sometimes place in the same category as mathematical necessity, reckoning them as parts of the mathematical process and not of the data. But the transfer of that crutch of our understanding which we call necessity, and which is really *implicitness*, to the ' laws ' of the behaviour of things, is sheer confusion. A ' law ' is merely a description of the way in which things are observed to act ; and there is not even the slightest similarity between that behaviour and the apodeictic implicitness of our logical and mathematical relations. In fact, that description of behaviour, that observation from experience and experiment, is always required by the mathematician or logician, as a part of his data ; it can never be evolved by deduction. The attribution of necessity to events arose long ago as a mythological idea ; events, instead of being regarded as manifestations, signs, of power, were imagined to be, on the contrary, *subject to* some power which the Greeks called Moira, or Fate ; Christian science slightly altered that pagan interpretation by saying that they ' obey laws.' To-day, when mythological ideas have lost much of their force, this is translated in most minds by imagining that, although we are not able to perceive the ' necessity ' of things behaving as they do, that behaviour is nevertheless determined by a necessity similar to the implicitness which we call logical necessity ; a view which is confirmed as, with the expansion of our knowledge, one or several laws become subsumed under more general laws, as, for instance, Boyle's law under the laws of thermodynamics. There is of course no perceivable ' necessity ' why stones should fall to the ground instead of flying upwards or remaining suspended in mid-air. And the circumstance that they always do fall to the ground, or that they will always do so throughout eternity, does not make the behaviour one whit more ' necessary.'

Even that uniformity, which is loosely identified with necessity, is only quite relatively known. Suppose—there is nothing extravagant in the supposition—that the laws of nature, the law of gravitation, say, were in process of slow modification through the ages, so that the gravitational behaviour of things would not be quite the same now as it was ten million years ago ; we should be quite incognizant of the fact, and should have no means of discovering it.

It is otherwise, however, with the principle of *causality*, viz., that everything must have a cause—as distinguished from the principle of *causation*, viz., that similar causes produce similar effects. *That* depends entirely upon *logical* necessity ; and it introduces that logical necessity into the entire universe. It introduces that necessity into the whole universe because every event in the universe is, by that principle, determined by the state of the universe at the preceding moment, this again by that of the moment before, and so on through an infinite regression ; so that nothing can happen that is not implicit in the state of the universe at any preceding time, at its very beginning, if we suppose it to have had a beginning. And it is this ' necessity,' this determinism, which is the great logical obstacle to the concept of freedom in the particular case of the events of our minds.

This necessity which attaches to the principle of causality, and which imposes a rigid determinism not on psychological events only, but on all events, not on the events of this universe only, but of all possible and imaginable universes, is a logical necessity, that is, it is, like all necessity, a feature of our methods of cogitation ; and, as I propose to show, it is nothing else, and can never by any feat of legerdemain be transferred from the processes of our cogitation to the objects to which they are applied.

All cognitive experience being a sign of something else, implies a cause of which it is the effect ; hence the infinite regression of causality in time and also in being. While we have no concept by means of which the infinite regression in time can be arrested, the infinite regression in being is arrested by the concept of an efficient cause, a source of action, a power. That being reached as the cause of all action, there is no need to go farther. Logical necessity is attached to the principle of causality because to repudiate it would be to admit that a new accession of power could from time to time be introduced into the universe from outside it, that is, from nowhere ; or, in other words, that a new power could arise out of nothing and be created. Now since it must come from nowhere, that new power would have to create itself ; but in order to create itself it would first have to exist, and it cannot exist before it is created. In fine, the repudiation of the principle of causality, which is a form of the principle of conservation of substance, would amount to saying that A is at the same time A and not-A.

It is by virtue of that logical necessary causality that the mathematician is enabled to ' construct the universe,' certain data being supplied ; that is to say, he will deduce mathematically all the events of the universe, *if* he is supplied with the data at a given moment. He is able to perform that deduction because he can deal with quantities, and the total quantity of power remains, by logical necessity, unchanged. The claim to construct thus the universe is the declaration of universal determinism.

But in order to perform that deduction and to justify determinism, another assumption is necessary in the mathematician's data, in addition to the postulate of the conservation of substance, which is the *only* element of the problem to which logical necessity attaches. Not only must the *quantity* of power be given and invariable, but also the *quality* of that power must be given and invariable. By ' quality ' of power is meant the manner in which that power acts, the character or direction of its action. That quality includes not only all the *known* ' laws of nature,' but *all* the ' laws of nature,' known and unknown ; it includes not only a description of the behaviour of energy in every existing circumstance but also of its behaviour in any circumstance. In order to ' construct the universe '—and to justify determinism— those ' laws of nature ' must be (1) given, i.e. completely known, and they must be (2) invariable. Otherwise the task is impossible.

We have seen that we have no absolute guarantee that the ' laws of nature ' are invariable. Assuming them, however, to be invariable, they must also be completely known. If we knew *all* the laws of nature, we should have a complete description of the way in which power would act under any circumstances, a complete description of its quality. We do not possess that complete description, and failing that, we cannot proceed with our task of constructing the universe. Our knowledge of the laws of nature is limited to a certain set of conditions, and any departure from those observed conditions will entirely invalidate our application of those laws. Before the Newtonian formulation of the laws of gravitation, for instance, we were familiar with the law that bodies fall towards the ground. The behaviour of the moon and the sun constituted a breach of our law of gravitation ; they did not fall to the ground, whereas according to our law they should have done so. A wider and more accurate formulation of the law was necessary in order to show that the apparent breach was in fact a consequence of the mode of operation of gravitational force. The mode of reaction of living organisms is different from that of physical inorganic objects, and therefore constitutes a breach of physical and chemical laws as we know them ; therefore we do not know either the laws or the configuration of living matter completely enough to apply those laws.

Neither a variation in the laws of nature, nor a condition not provided for in our knowledge of them, constitutes a breach in the principle of causality ; for that does not depend upon the invariability of the quality, but of the quantity, of power. The former would constitute a breach in the principle of *causation*, and would wholly stultify our power of making use of its logical necessity. Under conditions entirely different from those in which our ' laws of nature ' have been formulated, two things may happen : (1) a complete change in the behaviour of power may take place so as to constitute a breach of the principle of causation ; or (2) the change in the behaviour of power may simply be correlated to the peculiarity of the conditions and be a function of the laws of nature as known in other conditions.

In order that our construction of the universe, that is to say, the proof of determinism, may be carried out, all those data are required. Not only the invariability of quantity, but also that of quality, is demanded; and, while the former is a logical necessity, the latter is not. Our logical deduction proceeds not only upon the postulate that no new power is surreptitiously introduced into our data, but also that that power will always tend in the same direction but for the modifications which are functions of varying configurations (this in mechanics is expressed by the first law of motion). But in circumstances differing from those from which our ' laws ' have been formulated the essential quality of that power—which we do not know—may result in a breach of known laws; and if a change should, under those conditions, take place in the quality itself of that power, so that its variability will cease to be *the same function* of the configuration, then, while the principle of causality will remain unaffected, our logical deduction by means of its ' necessity ' will be stultified; for a change will have taken place which will not be included in our data.

Failing complete data as to how our power is going to act under all circumstances, our ' necessity ' is left ' in the air,' a pure abstraction. And that ' necessity ' which we transfer from the principle of causality to events amounts purely to this—that any event is predicable provided *all* the factors of that event are known. That ' necessity ' does not apply merely to the universe as we know it, but to any universe that the most incoherent imagination can devise; it does not only apply to any event that we can observe, but also to the most thaumaturgic performance that can be conceived. It is a ' necessity ' which is infinitely elastic. With all the data supplied you can not only ' construct the universe,' but you can predict the acts of an inebriate god.

12

That ' necessity ' which is a character of every possible and impossible event is not a characteristic of any, and cannot therefore be opposed to any ' freedom ' which we can conceive. But to say that an event is ' necessary ' because from the total sum of its constituent factors it follows *necessarily*, is merely to say that having taken place it cannot not have taken place ; for included in the sum of its factors is the fact that the event will take place when all the *other* factors are given, that is, the event itself is one of the data of its own determination. That ' necessity ' does not lie in the event, but in our groping analytical apprehension of it ; it is not a character of any sequence, but a character of our cognitive processes, which we transfer to the object of their investigation. That ' necessity ' is an intellectual illusion.

The third and most concrete form of that illusion exercises an unacknowledged influence upon its more general aspects ; for psychical causation is tacitly assimilated to physical causation and suspected of being ' governed ' by the latter, which, being apprehended objectively, is assumed to be unconnected with any psychical values, and to proceed according to laws which are not those of psychical causation. That implication is brought to a sharp focus by scientific materialism.

Even dualism, except in its most extreme and mythological form, generally allows to-day psycho-physical parallelism, namely, that to every change in conscious processes there corresponds a change in the organism. But it then follows that, if the laws of physics and chemistry hold good in the physical organism, the sequence of mental events must inevitably conform to the laws of physics and chemistry. Any determinism to be found in the latter must likewise apply in the same degree to the events of consciousness.

When Victorian materialism emphasized that point of view the scientific outlook was considerably simpler and more sharply defined than it is to-day. ' Consider, for example,' Victorian science would point out, 'the movements of a planetary system. A planet is subject to innumerable perturbations ; besides the larger movements of revolution in its orbit and of rotation on its axis, it quivers and deviates in countless ways. But every one of those movements takes place in accordance with a definite and rigid law, which we are able to formulate, which is very simple, and which applies with mathematical accuracy. A planet cannot move the millionth part of an inch out of its course except in conformity with those laws ; its slightest quiver is mathematically expressible and deducible ; the precise position which it occupies at any moment is the mathematically exact resultant of rigidly operating relations, so that from the slightest disturbance we can with secure confidence deduce the nature of the disturbing cause, as did Le Verrier and Adams when they discovered the planet Uranus without setting eyes on it. Our own organisms are composed of exactly the same substances as the material world, and their atoms and molecules must therefore move in a manner as rigidly uniform as do the planets, although we are not able to observe those movements and to formulate their laws so fully. It follows that when we appear to choose a course of action according to the value of a feeling, an idea, a presentation, a thought, that is a delusion ; for the molecular phenomena in our organisms proceed according to laws which admit of no alternative. And we are driven to conclude that our material movements which are governed by the laws of physics and chemistry would take their course in exactly the same way as they do, and that we should behave exactly as we do, if we had no feelings, no ideas, and no thoughts.'

Apart from the numerous assumptions contained in that argument, Victorian science in propounding it ignored its own most glorious achievement. For by treating the molecular dynamics of living organisms as equivalent to the dynamics of a planetary system it

set aside the conception of evolution. It assumed that no
fundamental change has taken place in the behaviour of
natural energies during the evolution from the simpler
to the most highly organized forms of material configurations. We realize to-day much more vividly than could
have been done in the days of Liebig, Vogt, Huxley, and
Tyndall, that a very far-reaching evolution has taken
place in the conditions and constitution of material systems
between those observed in the movements of a planetary
system and those taking place in the molecular systems
of living matter. It is a far cry from the simple gravitational movements of the former to the complex intra-
molecular changes in the latter, and to draw conclusions
from the one to the other is, to say the least, highly
hazardous. But from the point of view which physical
science has now reached the two processes are not even
parallel and strictly comparable, and the conclusions of
Victorian materialism are not only hazardous but positively
inapplicable. Those ' laws of nature ' which are the
formulas for the movements of large masses, the laws of
gravitation, of molar dynamics, of hydrostatics, of pressures
and temperatures, of radiation, appear to us to-day in
the light of *statistical* laws, of resultant averages ; and their
simplicity, their uniformity, are but the total effect of a
multitude of minute actions which are themselves neither
uniform nor simple, but infinitely varied. The laws of
intra-molecular changes are not the laws of observable
molar changes, which result from the mutual neutralization
of molecular actions into a simple and uniform average.
Those molecular actions—assuming the ultimate quality, or
' law,' of their constituent energy to be itself invariable—
must vary according to the internal constitution of molecular systems, which is becoming exceedingly complex.
The simpler the molecule, the simpler and more ' uniform '
its action ; the more complex the molecule, the greater
the variation in effects produced by very small causes,
the greater, that is, the deviation of the system from the

statistical law. The ultimate character of the constituents tells on the result in proportion to the complexity.

The fundamental conditions and constitution of the protoplasmic system of energy are admittedly as unknown to us as in the nineteenth century, but the progressive complexity lability, and instability, that have led up to it are more fully apprehended. Whatever our ignorance of the exact chemical and physical conditions of living matter, the very fundamental difference which I have pointed out, namely, that by virtue of the power of rebuilding the configuration of energy destroyed in each reaction a living system is the only one in which a reaction can be repeated and modified, is an observable fact. That circumstance alone precludes the assimilation of the organic molecular system to the planetary or any other inorganic system, for the difference between them is precisely that the one can be modified and the other cannot. That modification which does not take place in inorganic systems, is the concomitant of feeling, and of presentations which are modifications of feeling.

Our behaviour is modified by feeling and can be modified by presentations, and it is that relation which constitutes psychic causation or ' freedom.' The causal values of presentations differ completely from the causal values of molar physical factors, but there is no valid ground for supposing that they therefore differ from the physical causal values of biochemical factors ; for to the difference in the physical conditions and configurations of those factors there must needs correspond a difference in their causative action. Travelling to a given place in a strange country, I come upon cross-roads ; I turn to the right, but after proceeding a little way I meet an inhabitant and gather from him that I should have turned to the left. I retrace my steps and follow the other road. The changes in the movements of my body are physical events quite similar to the perturbations of the planet Neptune, and the whole process, like the astronomical

disturbance, can be considered from first to last as a purely
physical process, every psychical aspect being eliminated.
But if that process of redistribution of energy be considered
thus, it will be found that the causal values of the factors
are entirely transformed. In terms of massive events
and of observable physical laws there is no expressible
relation between the waves impinging on my tympanum
and the changes in my movements. The sounds may
be shrill or deep, high or low, short or prolonged, the
articulations may be those of Dutch, Greek, or Arabic
words ; instead of being spoken, they may be written in
black on a green board, or in green on a black stone—provided the words are understood, the result will be exactly
the same. The process to which that physical cause gives
rise in the organism is not only unlike the process of
gravitation or any other molar event, it is, in a sense,
the exact opposite. The physical effect of sound-waves
on a molar mass, and in fact on the membrane of the
tympanum, is a series of harmonic vibrations, the factors
of which are the tension, elasticity, weight, etc., of the
vibrating mass ; that is, the whole process depends on
the summation of the elements of the mass affected,
just as the gravitational force acts on the planet as if
the total mass of its varied elements were concentrated
at the centre. Whereas that process is the result of
a statistical levelling down of a multitude of molecular
actions to an average, the organic process is the outcome
of a series of *selective* reactions, in which the resultant
direction is determined by the choice by each element
of one direction of action out of a number of possible
directions. The cells of the auditory organs select certain
of the impinging waves ; the cells of the auditory centres
select certain effects of the auditory stimulus, and select
the path of their transmission to the cells of the speech
centre ; these further select the paths of association with
other sensory and motor centres ; and finally a selected
group of motor cells selects the paths of motor stimulation

to certain muscles, the coordinated contractions of which give rise to the modification of molar motion. That process is the reverse of the molar reaction ; instead of the diverse activities of the elements being statistically integrated into an algebraical average, so that their differences are eliminated in the combined result, the physical stimulus is, on the contrary, redistributed among a succession of highly differentiated elements, so that it is transformed into the specialized activity of those several elements. Those intricate selective actions and special-izations are themselves the outcome of countless similar selective actions reaching back to the beginnings of life. Owing to the continuity of those reactions, which are successive modifications of one another, the entire past of the organic system is coordinated with the actual, or active, present impulse which tends in a given direction. A complete transformation of the values of the external physical impulse is thus effected.

The old joke about the ' movements of molecules being transformed into feelings ' is a metaphysical chestnut which has ceased to be amusing ; what is transformed into feeling is not, of course, the movements of anything, but the causes of movements, that is, impulses to move-ment, and that is equally true in physics and in psychology. ' Moving particles ' are but the sensorily conceived signs of the sources of action. To imagine that your thoughts and your behaviour must be ' governed ' *either* by the ' laws ' of physics and chemistry *or* by your feelings and presentations, is a mere muddled assumption compounded of secular misconceptions. What ground have you for supposing that the two are different and must have different results ? The ' laws ' of chemistry and physics are but the description of the behaviour of objects ; no observation or description of the behaviour of molecular matter in living objects is available. It must, according to the principles of physical causation, and does in fact, as evidenced by the molar behaviour of living organisms, differ radically from our observed and described inorganic behaviour. That difference is, according to physical principles, a function of the difference in configuration of the systems ; it may be the same function of that difference as in inorganic systems, or it may be a quite different function. In the first case the organic behaviour would be describable as a ' law ' from a complete knowledge of organic configurations and our knowledge of inorganic physical and chemical ' laws ' ; in the other case new equations would be necessary in order to subsume both inorganic and organic laws under a more comprehensive formula. In either case there is no ground whatever for supposing that those ' laws ' of behaviour differ from those of psychical values.

That much is profoundly illusory in the apparent determination of behaviour by the forms of consciousness is what has been repeatedly emphasized in the present work. All those processes which constitute our consciousness can but give effect to impulses which actuate us and which are not themselves conscious. But that the modifications brought about by affective and cognitive values really correspond to the relations which those values bear in consciousness—and that relation constitutes the whole of our intuition of freedom—is a fact which is not invalidated by any of the arguments upon which necessitarian conceptions are founded.

CHAPTER VIII

THE PRIMARY CONATIVE TENDENCY

THE tendency and character of those forces which cause our actions and the phenomena of our consciousness are only known to us by their effects as our behaviour, and by their affects as our feelings. From those concrete and particular manifestations we may, by a process of inductive generalization, describe the ' character ' of animated beings in the same manner as we describe the ' properties ' of inorganic substances. From the fact that we are pleasantly affected by certain auditory experiences, say, and unpleasantly by others, we are led to say that we like music and dislike noise in general. Our self-knowledge, like all our knowledge, proceeds from the particular to the general. And we have no other ground than such inductions for any general description of the impulses which actuate us, and which are as obscure to us as is the general tendency—the absolute tendency, or ' first law of motion '—of the forces which give rise to chemical or electrical phenomena.

By a wider generalization all the tendencies manifested in behaviour appear to fall pretty obviously into two classes according as they have regard to the interests of the individual himself or to other, extra-individual, interests. The latter can be, and usually are, subsumed under the former. In order to act as a *motive* at all every value must be an individual value, every interest must assume the form at least of an individual interest. There can be no such thing as a purely altruistic motive ; from the moment that any consideration should show itself as wholly and purely altruistic it would thereby cease to be a motive. It is accordingly easy to show that every altruistic or extra-individual motive reduces itself to a form of individual interest. Thus the function of procreation, the type of a racial, extra-individual impulse, with all the extreme individual sacrifices which it entails, is really governed by an individualistic interest, and may be regarded as an assertion of individual power, an impulse to perpetuate the character, the type, of the individual. All ethical altruism is readily explained as enlightened self-interest ; all other-regarding motives are reducible to terms of egoism, and can be shown to present themselves in fact as more or less direct forms of egoism in order to operate as individual motives. The supremest sacrifice must appeal in some manner to the individual that makes it ; he does, after all, nothing but what he likes. All conduct, whether on the human or on the animal plane, is interpretable in terms of egoism, and is constantly so interpreted with a logic which embarrasses refutation.

That interpretation is painfully confirmed by our familiarity with the prodigies of human selfishness. We see men hacking their way to what they deem their personal advantage regardless of every other consideration, paving the path of their cupidity with the lives of their fellows. We know the appalling crudity and cruelty of ultimate conscious motives, and we know also something of the egoism that disguises itself under hypocritical professions and sentiments. We are easily led to conclude that the human world, no less than the animal world which is red in tooth and claw, is, to be perfectly honest, a manifestation of pure, savage, ruthless, cruel egoism, and that to pretend that it is otherwise is but an attempt to throw mawkish sentimental dust into our eyes.

And yet, in spite of that seeming obviousness, a more fundamental consideration will, I believe, show that if the two orders of motive tendencies be reducible to one, it is not at all under the head of egoism, but under that of extra-individual impulses, that they are subsumable. An ambiguity lies at the root of the egoistic interpretation. The distinction between self-regarding and other-regarding impulses does not at all correspond to what we commonly term selfishness and altruism. It is, of course, a dynamic necessity that all motives whatsoever, in so far as they are conscious at all, should appeal to the individual in terms of his interests. He does what satisfies his impulses, and in so far acts egoistically ; and no motive which is effective can escape from the circle of that egoism. But it does not at all follow that those motivating impulses are therefore self-regarding in their tendency. The actual goal of the impulses which actuate us is, as we have seen, not represented in consciousness ; what is present in consciousness as the ' motive ' of action, the satisfaction sought, is something quite different from that goal. There is no impulse in living nature more blindly selfish than that of sexual love ; it is ruthless and unscrupulous, it operates as an egoism more self-centred than hunger. There is no instance in nature of more cynical callousness than the sadic love of the bee or the spider. And yet that impulse is the clearest and most direct manifestation of an impulse which is race-regarding, and which utterly subordinates the individual to the race, sets him aside and unflinchingly sacrifices him to the race-purpose. The man who sacrifices all his human ties and obligations in order to follow the imperious behest of an obsessing idea is judged a selfish man. But the impulse that animates him is of the most intensely extra-individual import. The satisfaction of the impulses of the individual is not by a very long way the same thing as the *advantage* of the individual. To imagine that the two are identical is the grossest possible misunderstanding of the most fundamental and elementary facts of psychology.

That the individual acts ' selfishly ' or ' altruistically ' is no criterion of the self- or other-regarding nature of

the impulse that urges him. The presented value of the
motive in individual consciousness and the character of
the impulse he obeys are two quite different things. We
now know that the urge of the impulses which actuate
living organisms is, so far as the consciousness of the
organism is concerned, blind, and that the form of conscious
' motive ' under which they may present themselves to
consciousness has nothing whatever to do with the
direction of their tendency, their teleological value.
That an individual acts from a motive which is to him
purely selfish is no criterion of the end and utility of the
impulse which actuates him. His own attitude may be,
and in most cases is, grossly and frankly egoistic, but the
value of his selfish impulse may at the same time be purely
that of a race-interest. The moral psychologist is fond
of gushing sloppy sentiment on the maternal instincts of
the hen. Does anyone seriously suppose that the hen is
actuated by sloppy sentiments ? Does anyone, *a fortiori*,
suppose that she has any conception of the ' interest of
the race ' ? She is actuated by no sentimental or theoretical considerations, but by impulses that are ' blind,'
that is to say, unpresented in consciousness except by
instant feelings of pleasantness or unpleasantness. That
in no way alters the fact that this blind impulse is
indubitably related to ends in which the individual hen
counts for nothing, and which have regard to a horizon
of life-purposes in which her ' interests ' are irrelevant.

Nor is the contrast one between the cruelty of selfishness, and the loving-kindness and self-sacrifice of altruism.
As a fact the race-impulse can be, and usually is, a
thousand times more cruel, more callous and more ruthless,
than any individualistic egoism. What we associate with
the heartless cruelty of nature—her disregard of the
individual—is a manifestation of racial, of extra-individualistic impulses. There is nothing more cruel than the
' altruism ' of extra-individual impulses.

The crudest individual impulse of life, the ' instinct

of self-preservation,' may, on the other hand, be quite opposed to the individual's interests, may be so even manifestly in his own consciousness and judgment. The man condemned beyond hope to utter misery and suffering, and impotent uselessness, even while clearly realizing his situation, clings to life, and calls himself a coward for so doing.

All creative activities are pursued in general in a purely selfish spirit ; the artist, the creator, seeks the satisfaction of certain cravings for expression and perfection of production, sacrificing many things to that individual satisfaction, discarding the call of obligations. But that true expression and creative work should take place is not the interest of the individual, but of the race ; the artist's, the scientist's, the philosopher's stake in their work is as nothing compared to the stake in it of the race. All art is race-regarding in its nature ; it is one of the most essential elements and means of the education, the development, the evolution of the race. The share represented by the individual satisfaction of the artist, obtained at the cost of pangs and travails that seem to consume his very life, is as nothing beside its value to the race. His labour is at once as selfish and as altruistic as the mother's care for her offspring.

The writings of Freud and Jung have of late popularized the notion that many manifestations of conative, affective, imaginative activity are transformed aspects of the sexual instinct—or, as it would be more correct to say, of the reproductive instinct, for sexuality is only a special form of it. That notion was familiar enough to psychologists before Freud. It is a matter of easy observation that in many cases religious emotion, artistic, intellectual emotion and creative activity, are interchangeable with the manifestations of the reproductive instinct. They take its place and it may take theirs. They are channels along which flow the same ultimate forces, which appear to assume now one form and now another. The ecstasis of the religious mystic gives expression to reproductive impulses which his or her asceticism holds suppressed ; and in the more morbid forms of religious hysteria the intimate connection is revealed beyond the possibility of mistake. So all art, all the highest forms of pictorial expression, of poetry, of emotional literature, all music, are suffused with the eternal theme of sexual love. They are, like the displays of colour and song in animals, expressional manifestations of the same impulse which perpetuates the species. To the Oriental, whose vision is not veiled by the primness of our conventions, all our art and music appear at their face-value for what they are—purely erotic. The whole affective life of man is coloured with the hues of those emotions which naturally associate themselves with the transmission of life, with the race-impulse in the most concrete aspect of its function.

Rather than say, as we have been in the habit of saying, that those manifestations are disguised sublimations of the sexual impulse, it would be more exact to say that the whole range of creative manifestations, together with those which have more directly to do with the reproductive functions, are all aspects and forms of the one primary impulse. Artistic or mystic emotions are not ' transformed ' or ' disguised,' or ' sublimated ' concupiscence, but various manifestations of an impulse which is the common source of all. They have the common character that they are in their import and scope race-regarding, other-regarding, extra-individual, impersonal evolutionary impulses. In all those activities the individual is the instrument of the evolutionary forces of the race and of Life.

The artist, the thinker, the scientist, are occupied with aims which concern the race more than the individual, which are not ephemeral and contingent, but abiding. They are engaged in creating the racial mind, the future— a creative, a reproductive act in no less strict a sense than the bringing forth of a human organism. The artist is consumed with a desire to express himself ; and what is that act of expression but the communication to others, to the race, of what he accounts most valuable in his field of vision ? What is the goal of that impulse but the impregnation of the mind of humanity with his own ? However solitary and self-absorbed his labours, however isolated and insulated his thought—and with the jealousy of a lover the true thinker ever seeks to insulate thus his creative act from all contamination—it is to the race, to humanity, to the future, that, unknown though it be to himself, what his mind brings forth is addressed. What concern has he in the past or in the future of humanity, in its redemption, in truth, in sounding the abysses of universal questions ? What's Hecuba to him or he to Hecuba ? Those interests hold him, possess him, obsess him ; he enjoys the little honorary, nominal fees of joy in his work, pride in it, the little pleasures of vanity ; or suffers with equal readiness the insults of ignorance and stupidity, the scorns of the unworthy, the rancour of prejudice, and the patronage of fatuous misunderstanding. Paltry fees, and squalid martyrdoms ! Assuredly they are not and cannot be weighed as factors in the motive powers that urge him to consume the inmost energies of his life. A far deeper, more potent force, despotically impels him unknown to himself, as it impels the gnat to give its life in an embrace.

No creative act, no real work at all, is in its nature self-regarding. Indeed, as in his creative acts, so in the whole of his activities, the individual is moved by forces which are equally unperceived by him, and which use him merely as their instrument to ends that extend far beyond his sight. Those forces, in fact, care little at all for the individual ; those cosmic forces treat the individual with utter disregard and indifference. That he should be impelled to ' self-preservation,' that he should cling to life, to the means of existence, that he should

seek to extend his powers and assert himself in his generation, are necessary conditions of his acting at all. But
never does he find it possible to live by that bread alone ;
the values of life bear the hues of aims which extend
out of the sight of the individual. Confine him within
the circle of that self-preservation, and he inevitably
pines, mortally suffocated. Feed him, warm him, shelter
him, ' preserve ' him, furnish him with all the necessaries
of individual life, and he will go mad or commit suicide.
Creation, were it but the crude reproduction of his own
kind, becomes, in the absence of any other manifestation
of the life-force, the centre of all life's values. To those
creative ends, to those evolutionary ends, are his self-
preservation, his clingings to every straw of life, subsidiary
and subservient. And when the powers of racial use and
import are exhausted, when he has ceased to be in mind
and spirit creative, even the self-preservative life-instinct
as a rule vanishes or becomes enfeebled ; his clinging
grasp relaxes, and he is ready to take his departure.

It is, when properly considered, a rather preposterous
notion that those forces which act through the individual,
of whose real import and end he is totally unconscious,
whose origin lies in a remote and long regression of
evolutionary development, are in the least concerned
with the individual, are in any respect individual-regarding.
Such a conception appears, when we come to face fairly
its prodigious impertinence, as the anti-climax of anthropo-
centrism.

Those diversified impulses that make up our ' being '
are the stratified accumulation of the concrete forms
assumed by the primal tendencies of life under the
operation of affective and cognitive experience. Not one
of those forms is itself innate and original ; all are
necessarily developed in reaction to feeling and cognition ;
all are necessarily ' acquired.' Without affective and
cognitive experience no concrete appetence, no specific
impulse, can arise at all. Hunger, for instance, is beyond

dispute not primary ; it is a special developed instinct of plasmophagous animality ; it is unknown to the quietly and continuously breathing and light-absorbing plant-life out of which animality became differentiated. Love is no less an acquired instinct ; sexuality is not primary, but a developed adaptation, a division of labour. The breath itself, the spirit, is not primal ; there are organic forms which do not breathe oxygen—saprophytic bacteria, yeasts, that contrive to metabolize by way of fermentative processes and dispense quite well with air. Not one impulse of life can be discerned to be primary, innate, original, and inseparable from the attributes of life.

The distinction between self-regarding and other-regarding impulses does not appear to exist at the origin of life. In plant-life structural provisions and reactions for self-preservation would seem, with a few rare excep-tions, as in sensitive plants, to be entirely absent. The plant does not protect itself, shows no defensive instincts, evinces, so far as structural provisions and behaviour indicate, no objection to dying. Its structural reactions, its organic cunning, are, on the contrary, wholly directed towards reproduction ; individual-regarding provisions and impulses would not appear to exist in the original disposition of life. Extra-individual impulses have not been, it would seem, evolved by a process of sublime sentiment from a fund of original egoism, but on the contrary, they are the dominant, original impulses of life ; and it is self-preservation, the individualistic impulse, which has been derived out of them. Self-preservation, like hunger, is probably a special invention and attribute, a sort of perverted instinct, of predatory, cannibalistic, combative animality. The instinct of self-defence has arisen as a correlative of the instinct of attack.

Whatever the nature of that tendency which constitutes the quality of the impulses of life, it is clear that it is not concerned chiefly with the individual. The problems of behaviour present themselves to us accordingly under

a new aspect. For individualistic philosophy the problem was, ' How can extra-individual motives arise out of individual motives ? ' For us the problem is rather, ' How can individual motives arise out of extra-individual motives ? What is the nature of egoism in an organism which is entirely ruled by impersonal forces that care nothing for the individual ? '

There are certain types of behaviour, thrust prominently upon our notice in the present phase of human development and social order, to which we refer by the words ' selfishness,' ' egoism.' In order to understand those types of behaviour we must regard them in a somewhat different light from that in which we are accustomed to view them. Egoistic behaviour is *not* merely behaviour resulting from motives of self-interest, for all motives, in order to act at all, must appeal to individual interest ; that is the condition of their operation. It is *not* merely behaviour characterized by callousness, cruelty, defect of sympathy ; some of the most purely extra-individual impulses exceed all others in cynical cruelty, in the complete absence of the feeling of sympathy. The behaviour which we call selfish and egoistic is certainly not characterized, or psychologically explained, by those descriptions. It is a pathological condition consisting in a particular atrophy and degeneration associated with otherwise advanced conditions of development.

The crudity of egoism which we lament, and which is sometimes ascribed to ' human nature,' is the product of certain conditions, namely, the structure and mode of evolution of our social order, on which is imposed strife, conflict, as a supreme law. A consuming disease is thereby engendered—*panic fear*, which is the ruling emotion in all competitive conditions. In the social psychology thus created by the organization of terrorism, the defensive, self-preservative instincts are naturally, as in hunted beasts, stimulated to the utmost and suffer from a chronic pathological hypertrophy. We are sometimes naïvely surprised to discover that the self-making man who coldly employs himself in crushing human lives on a large scale and despoiling widows and orphans is, in his family circle, the mildest and tenderest of men, acutely affectionate and sensitive. Naturally ; it is the social order alone which evokes the pathological reaction of the self-preservative instincts—not ' human nature.' The general result of that hypertrophy is that all other tendencies and affections are stunted, starved, atrophied. When he has secured himself and satisfied his animal instincts, the victim of panic has no interests in this life, and his tastes and satisfactions are those of a Hottentot or a baboon. It is that atrophy which manifests itself in the baseness, the vulgarity, the sottishness of the mentality associated with our commercialism. It is worse than wicked, it is vulgar. It produces not so much indignation as disgust. The likes and dislikes of the competitive animal are bestial.

Self-preservative egoism is developed, like every instinct in life, in response to the need for it ; the greater danger of attack, the greater the operation of self-defence, of self-preservation. And the result is the amputation by the stress of fear of all the higher forms of conation, and the reduction of the individual and of the race to a state of evolutionary destitution in which they are left shrivelled and withered down to the basis of the crudest and basest forms of instinct. Fear, self-preservation, self-defence, are *negative* instincts whose function is mere escape and avoidance ; they can never accomplish, achieve, create anything, they can never give rise to any development, any evolution. It is not the hypertrophy of self-preservation, but the consequent *atrophy* of developmental forces, which constitutes the baseness of egoism.

We come here upon a distinction of the most momentous import. We use, and must continue to use, the words ' base,' ' noble,' ' lower,' ' higher,' in reference to various forms and manifestations of the conative impulses of life. That is to say, we assign *values* to the principles of valuation themselves, evaluate them as determinants of ' higher ' or ' lower ' orders of value. On what ground do we do so ? What justification have we for stigmatizing the pleasures of the swine and exalting those of the hero or the thinker ? Are they not all equally manifestations of life's conative impulse ?

On that question we must not allow ourselves to be put off with vague justifications. It is upon it that the validity of our evaluations must rest.

It is, I trust, clear that within the human organism in its psychological aspect are included in a wide series of evolutionary stratifications diverse forms of particularized impulses which reach back through the whole regress of human ancestry to the primordial reactions of the first protists, and represent in the dispositions of the human individual the entire psychological evolution that has led up to it. Psychological evolution, that is, the unfolding of the conative impulses of life, tentatively feeling their way to more approximate realizations of their tendencies, is exactly similar in the outline of its course to organic evolution. Schematically mapped out, that course assumes the form of a branching genealogical tree. Some of the branches diverge from near the roots into a line of limited success to which they remain committed ; many thousands of various lines branch off at different levels, representing specialized forms of activity which confine the conative forces within a determined channel and exclude them from any other form of expression. One great branch, that of the articulates, represents what seemed the great achievement of an efficient method, the fixation by successive elaborations and accumulations of its minutest details in rigid hereditary structure of instinctive behaviour. The main trunk is composed of the more indefinite, unstable, and labile types which are constantly inveigled into side-lines of specialization, while the remnant goes on unsettled, open to new opportunities and routes towards a truer expression, and finds in humanity a new outlet of enormously diversified choice and variability. The results of human evolution itself are not structurally fixed at all, they are not inheritable, but precariously transmitted by the social organism. So that the human individual, left to himself, remains a mere brute, on the level of the crudest animality out of which mankind has arisen. For the human stage of evolution he is entirely dependent on social heredity ; it may leave him in the palæolithic phase of human evolution or raise him to the level of the highest attained development.

Now it is a fact that where, in the individual consciousness, various forms belonging to different strata of psychological evolution exist side by side, their relation in the evolutionary scale is immediately felt in consciousness. The older, more primitive and rudimentary organic impulses pertaining to ancient and simple stages of psychological development, fixed mostly as physiological needs or wild instincts, are directly *known as lower*. Where in the same consciousness there exist more recent, freer, more highly developed needs, desires, appetences, these, whether prepotent or no, will infallibly be recognized as of higher value than the lower.

That intuition is not some mystic and mysterious sense. It is the natural and inevitable result of the operation of the conative impulses of life. If we have succeeded in conceiving that impulse as perpetually tending towards expression in a determined direction, it follows that the affective values expressed in consciousness which are most advanced in the direction towards which it is tending are more complete expressions of it than those corresponding to its more rudimentary and primitive expressions. The satisfaction of the impulse of life in its later achievements in self-development may not be more 'massive' than that derived from the more primitive forms of its needs—the latter are

more firmly established and perfected in function and
feeling—but it is necessarily of higher quality. And that
quality, that value is directly recognized as higher where
it is felt at all.

There are natural values. So enormous a proportion
of our values are manifest and transparent forgeries,
traditional fabrications arising out of the power-relations
of the social order, that we have in general grown dis-
trustful of the validity of all values. That is the penalty
of our ancestral dishonesties, the Nemesis of human lies.
But those forged values could not have arisen at all had
there been no sterling currency; there are originals to
those forgeries. The whole activity of life consists in
reaction to the affective values determined by its conative disposition; and among those values themselves there
exist relations, a respective value of values, a hierarchical
order of evolutionary rank, which is intuitively known—
albeit frequently confounded with, and obscured by,
traditional pseudo-values. ' Higher ' means the closer
approximation of the conative tendency that determines
all activities to its intrinsic goal.

The word ' conscience ' in its old acceptation, has,
together with all its aliases, ' moral sense,' ' innate
intuition,' ' categorical imperative,' dropped to all intents
and purposes out of our vocabularies. We no longer
believe in any innate, arbitrary and absolute foundation
and final dogmatic appeal of ethics. Morality, it has
become unmistakably clear, is a social product, frequently
a social convention, frequently a fabricated social lie.
When our ' conscience ' prompts adherence, deference to
that convention, the instinct, the ' still small voice,' is
no other than our ' fear of public opinion,' our lapping
up of current shibboleths and consecrated judgments.
It is not noble and divine, but essentially ignoble and
ovine. It pertains to the instinct cowardice. The
concept of ' conscience ' is now wholly discredited and
obsolete.

Nevertheless I do not fear to affirm that there exists a real and momentous fact, which, if not strictly identical with the ancient concept, is at any rate analogous. Not certainly a 'moral sense,' an instinctive intuition of ethics, but in a considerably wider sense an innate evaluation of all values.

The relations which we term ethical arise out of the peculiar condition of human development which, depending entirely on that of the social aggregate, require *as a condition of that development* the mutual adjustment of the elements of that aggregate; and it is that essential adjustment, which cannot be carried out here by organic equilibrium, which is the all-important object of ethical growth. But that ethical adjustment is but a part of the process of development of the powers of life, and exists only *as a means towards it.* Hence the ethical aspect, as it is currently understood, namely, as concerned with human relations, is but a limited, partial and subsidiary aspect of the aims which represent the ever widening goals towards which the forces of life tend and aspire.

Wherever various orders of values stand side by side in consciousness, the higher by the side of the lower, that relative order is recognized and directly known, whether admittedly or no. And that sense of value, however confused by traditional pseudo-values, is not to be wholly accounted for by reference to those, for it most potently and clearly asserts itself when operating in utter defiance of convention and tradition, of 'public opinion,' of established norms. It is most conspicuous— for then it is the most genuine and direct expression of conation towards higher levels of realization—when isolated, obstructed, decried and defiant. By virtue of that natural sense of value it is that we appeal to *our own approval* as to the highest, most valid and competent court.

The highest that is in us is recognized, known, as highest, however faintly felt, to whatever order that 'highest' may appertain.   The Christian who is debarred by his educational misfortune from seeing beyond the thick veil of traditional spiritual values, of traditional ' truth,' yet cannot but strongly feel, and justly, the enormous superiority, the transcendent worth, of those spiritual values above the coarseness, crudity, bestiality, ' materialism,' of the world about him, of the lower values he knows.   Hence his ' conscience ' adds the full might of its judgment to the already titanic force of established values with which he has been endowed by his educational growth, to the ' cloud of witnesses,' and confirms them into an immovable rock of faith.   The force of natural values confirms that of artificial ones, pronounces them to be immeasurably the highest that he knows.   All higher values, which he only knows by hearsay, are confounded by him, and assimilated with, that crudeness and ' materialism ' to which his conscience infallibly declares him to be superior.

The highest that is felt is confidently known as highest. Hence, as we have noted, satisfaction within the sphere of the base can only arise from atrophic development, from *absence* of the higher forms of conation.   Our vulgarity is not a development of baseness, but a deficiency of higher development.   Every form of degradation is the conversion of means into an end in itself, a limitation ; every means tends to' become an end and to bar the way to further outlook in the absence of evolutionary activity. Physical force, money, food, talent, scholarship, self-preservation, ' morality,' become ends in themselves, and development is thereupon arrested.

The pervasive and multiform animal instinct which is in some of its partial aspects described as ' self-regarding sentiment ' is, I consider, much more fundamental ; it is a feeling of evolutionary values.   Protean in the multiplicity of its forms and manifestations, it is like all other impulses, subject to aberrations and degradations, and to developmental sublimations.   The strutting of all males before females, their display of themselves, their outspreading of feathers and colours, their songs and gurgles, and comical love-dances and parades, are, on the face of them, immediately related to the reproductive race-function, that is, to the most obviously extra-individualistic impersonal impulse. They are in that aspect the very reverse of self-regarding. Yet they are at the same time the type of self-regard, of vanity, of exaltation of self, self-admiration and desire for admiration. What is here admired, what is held up as an object of complacency and admiration for others, for the females especially as instruments of propagation and perpetuation, is not ' self ' at all, the ' ego,' the ' subject ' of metaphysics. Does anyone mean to tell me that a stickleback or a turkey has any concern for his metaphysical ' ego ' ? The object of admiration, of vanity, is the achievement of the life-impulse, the perfection with which it has realized itself, attained to expression in the individual. The individual displays his strength, his agility, his talents, his accomplishments, his beauty ; he does not display his weakness, his foibles, his cowardice, his ugliness ; he hides those. He does not display his *self*, he displays as admirable what he regards as most exalted in his composition, carefully putting out of sight and forgetting those ingredients which have base values. His struttings are an æsthetic judgment of values, a declaration of faith in what he considers to be admirable. And all our æsthetics, our poetic, musical, pictorial arts, are, as is commonly recognized, derivative transformations of male love-struttings and displays. (Compare the general inaptitude of women for creative art. The creatively artistic woman is an abnormality, subject to ovarian abnormalities. Sappho, the archetype of the woman artist, suffered from perverted sexuality. On the other hand, woman is the great appreciator and enjoyer of art, if not a judge and a critic of it.)

Vanity, conceit, pride, the wooing of public admiration, are exaltations not of self, but of those aspects of self which individuals at various stages of evolution regard as the most admirable in themselves, the highest. They display for public admiration those qualities to which their outlook, whether limited or developed, ascribes the highest values. Those qualities may be precisely those which they themselves possess in the smallest degree, which they not so much possess as would like to possess ; they boast of that which they have not. The coward makes a display of courage, the ugly man of beauty, the weak of power. ' Hypocrisy is an homage which vice pays to virtue.'

All ' sentiment of self,' self-admiration, ostentation, implies a scale of valuations, a differentiation of the qualities and aspects which are held up to the admiration of self and others. ' Those values,' it may be objected, ' are social products—we pride ourselves on what others admire, envy in us ; the female *selects* the male ; ostentation courts public opinion.' Is not that a vicious circle ? What determines the selection of the female, of public opinion, of others ? The approval of others is courted when *that* is regarded as the highest judgment ; it is courted by the mediocre individual who is evolutionally not even up to the average level ; that is why most vanity and ostentation are base and vulgar. The higher individual, he who has developed, carried in himself the evolutionary development higher, does *not* court public opinion, but, on the contrary, defies it, scorns it, offends it. He opposes to it his valuations, and abides securely by that judgment. He seeks, on the contrary, to impose *his* valuations on public opinion, to impose ' his personality.' ' His personality ? ' It is, of course, no more his personality than that which the vulgar ostentator seeks to display, it is his highest values, the highest point of evolution reached by aspiring life within himself. He no more desires to display or impose his weaknesses, his lower values, than does the turkey.

CHAPTER IX

CONSCIOUSNESS AS A SOCIAL PRODUCT

THE 'human faculty,' suggestive in its portentous powers of a miraculous origin, rests upon a very definite fact—the symbolism of the word. Language is not, as was at one time supposed, the device invented by a transcendent intellect to achieve self-utterance ; it is the source whence that intellect itself has sprung into being. Word-symbolism created the human faculty. When once, out of cries, calls, and signals, the trick of naming was caught up, no limit could stay the course of abstraction, the coining of things, the acts and qualities of things, the qualities of those qualities, into words— permanently fixed concepts. From the naming of the trivial objects of its daily needs the human mind went on to 'universals' and lists of the 'categories.' There was nothing to arrest its career of predication and comparison, of analysis and synthesis. The system of symbols, accumulated and refined in acuteness by the interaction of human minds, became not only a system of signals between them, the means of communication, of education, of psychological transmission ; it also became the means of thought, the organ of human psychosis. Man's soul became symbolic. The word became man.

We think in words. Thought, the peculiar medium of human psychism, constitutes the great bulk of our focal consciousness, of what we term 'our mind.' That consciousness is to an overwhelming degree cognitive ; hence the identification by introspective psychology of mind, of soul, with thought—the *res cogitans* ; the intellectual, cognitive, epistemological conception of mind.

But cognition, we have more than once noted, does much more than afford the means of effectively serving the conative impulses of the organism ; it reacts upon those impulses themselves and transforms them. Under its action the primordial, undetermined psychic forces, conations, affections, take on new shapes, tend to new objectives, assume new values, are directed to new fields of action, to new horizons of desire. Only thus can those forces come into purposive operation ; their development is thus determined by that of cognition.

Hence not only has the word, by its analytic algebra, created a new cognitive organ, the intellect, and brought forth the marvels of its power ; it has no less amazingly called new purposes and new emotions into being ; it has opened a new world of aims and values. The animal whom the word had quickened began to shake and startle the world with the strange sounds of laughter and of tears. His purposes and values, his looking before and after, flew in their oscillations beyond the organic orbit of his daily needs until, by an appalling aberration, they swung beyond life itself, into eternity. Human desires, the things we live by, the things we live and die for, are no less than thought itself the offspring of the word. Armed with his symbolism, the thinking animal has become a moral animal, a religious animal, an artistic animal. Not the cognitive instrument alone is the product of the word. The word has created the very soul of man.

But there is another side to the picture. Against the prodigies of thought are to be set no less colossal miseries and handicaps ; against its triumphs its disasters. That symbolism has been the source of all human marvels but it is—a symbolism. Its whole structure, and consequently that of the thought and the mentality that is the outcome of it, is artificial, factitious. In proportion to its very perfection, to its power of abstract symbolization, it of necessity drifts more and more out of touch with that which it symbolizes, acquires a weird, unnatural self-existence apart from it. The word-fashioned concept, the Platonic ' Idea,' becomes a sort of entity endowed with an unnatural phantasmal life. In the dumb animal life and its cognitive exploration are miserably limited. But by that very limitation they are anchored to reality. The higher animals are capable of thought, and their thought is, like ours, symbolic ; but the symbols with them are the actual sensory signs of cognition. The purposes and values that grow out of that cognition spring directly from primordial conations. With word-symbolism man has become the master of a wonder-working machine ; but, as with every machine, its master has also become its slave. He has become overwhelmed by his own power. Thought is limed in the glue of words, and strives in vain to rise. It is compelled more and more to dwell in that symbolic world upon which it depends. Leaving the depths, the realities of psychic life behind, it is drawn to the iridescent film that plays upon the surface ; it comes to be a stranger to reality and shrinks when confronted with it as before something exotic and strange, as if it had seen a ghost The word-symbol tends to displace, to be mistaken for, and handled in lieu of, the idea, the experience for which it ostensibly stands. The magic power of creating substantive concepts, multiplied by the word, betrays by its fatal facility. Words can be struck without check from the multiplying-press, like treasury notes, and are no longer under the necessity of representing bullion in the bank of reality. They may even be forged, fabricated ; a false currency may be thrown into circulation, which even experts may find it difficult to distinguish from the legitimate tender of thought. How many of the ideas, of the thoughts within you, cling to the values which they professedly connote ? How many are demonstrable fabrications, the history of which, where and when they were coined, is even historically traceable ?

Out of that artificial life of word-thought, conceptual thought, out of that ' realism '—in the scholastic sense— strange antinomies have come about. By virtue of that power, man, the discoverer of truth, has become also the inventor of lies. *Homo sapiens*, the rational animal, is of all animals the only one that possesses the faculty of being inordinately, fantastically, deliriously irrational. He is so habitually, systematically, of set purpose. The dumb world, were it not itself unrational, would behold him with amazement commercing with phantasms, seeing things, gravely gibbering to himself, cogitating phantasmagorias, haranguing the void, orating to the east-wind, struck with unaccountable lunacies, stung to homicidal manias by hidden ecstasies, and so ardently dealing with his chimeras as to be entirely insensible to the realities about him. Did ever any sensible dumb animal woo life with such mummeries ? His thought weighs the stars, and he lives enchanted in a world of hallucinations. He is the master of thought and the fool of the universe.

The faculty of man has not only become the supreme instrument of adaptation, of evolutionary development, but also the means of inadaptation, of degradation, of degeneration. Man is the moral animal ; he is the creator of the ideals, he is the saint, the martyr, the hero. Yet he is also the basest of all animals He lays down his life for an ideal, and he cheats a child.

The dependence of the human mind upon word-symbolism carries with it the most extraordinary biological consequence. That psychical apparatus is physiologically intransmissible. For its handing down from one generation to another none of the physiological devices elaborated by organic evolution are available ; for through organic continuity no cognition can be transmitted. The transmission of human cognition can only take place by the operation of the social aggregate. It is the latter which supplies to every individual mind its word-consciousness. The soul of man, in so far as it is human at all, is a social product. His actuating impulses, the palimpsest of his instincts, his organism and sense-organs, derive from the multifarious parentage of his organic ancestry. His 'humanity' is entirely derived from the collective social environment, not by way of descent, but directly from the actual phase of social growth into which he is born. That human consciousness enters his being mainly by means of words, which carry with them all the developments, and all the diseases, anomalies, and falsifications of human word-thought. That word-consciousness post-natally implanted into each individual is superposed on all the products of pre-human psychological evolution, and becomes his focal consciousness, his thinking soul.

It is a strange situation. 'Humanity,' the social environment, the 'Spirit of the times'—the Hegelian *Zeitgeist*—are mere abstractions. We are in the habit of discounting the expressions as somewhat loose metaphors, personifications of concepts which have only a theoretical existence. They connote merely the aggregate, the resultant, the sum-total of constituent human units. There are no such things, you will be told; there are only *men*. And yet, as a fact, no individual human consciousness exists at all except as the product of that aggregate, of that 'abstraction.' The whole of human consciousness, not its word-language alone, but all the consequences of it, its concepts, its values, its sentiments, ideas and ideals, are imparted to each individual, who but for that artificial animation would be but a dumb ape, by that aggregate, that 'abstraction'—which is itself made up of traditionally, socially manufactured souls.

It is by that transmission that the individual can become the 'heir of all the ages,' and that human evolution is possible. But here also those great advantages are set off by no less colossal disadvantages. Not only are the achievements of the race transmissible to the individual, but so also are the diseases which in the social organism word-thought has accumulated. The basis of fact for the current prejudice against the intermarriage of kindred is that family taints and morbid tendencies are thereby summated and intensified. Precisely the same thing takes place in the social transmission of the human mind. Every accident and disease of thought is accumulated in that heredity no less, far more surely indeed, than are its conquests and achievements. That socially transmitted mind-stuff does not at all represent the actual experience and cognition of the race, the accumulated achievement of its effort to know its psychic development, its supreme conquests. What is transmitted to, and bestowed upon, the individual is something entirely different. It is not the psychological product of the intrinsic powers and constitution of the human mind, but that of the constitution of the social organism that transmits it.

The social organism—so we must call it, since it exercises the most important function of an organism, that of procreation—is yet no physiologically adjusted organism ; no automatic equilibrium has taken place within it. It is one of the fictions of all our ' history,' which has become embodied in our terminology and language—e.g., in the very words ' society,' ' social,' ' constitution '—that the human race has become ' organized,' has 'organized ' itself ; implying a purposive, deliberate, collective effort to contrive, dispose, and settle human relations in a practical manner, with a view to the best attainable result and efficiency, under the guidance of a will to truth. Nothing of the sort has ever taken place. Mankind has not organized itself or become organized. The ' social organism ' has been constituted by the self-establishment of dominating and predatory individual powers, which have subjugated the bulk of the race. That is the only sort of ' organization ' that has ever taken place in the ' social organism '—tyranny tempered by revolt. Consequently the mental inheritance transmitted to the individual is that transmitted by those established powers, and is not the psychological product of the ' human faculty ' or ' human nature,' but of those transmitting powers. It is not the product of cognitive impulses at all ; and cannot be psychologically regarded as representing cognition or experience. The impulses and interests under the urge of which it has been produced have not been those which throughout the development of life bring about cognition as a utilitarian function, but altogether different impulses and interests, those, namely, that have for their object the maintenance of power and domination, instincts of self-preservation. They have not been produced by will to truth, but by will to falsehood.

Hence the socially transmitted material of human consciousness is a profoundly falsified material consisting of pseudo-concepts, pseudo-distinctions, pseudo-values Every human mind born into the world receives that falsified mentality from the social environment, is educated by it, and provided with falsified metaphysics, falsified psychology, falsified history, falsified ethics. By a subtle and crowning falsification the process by which the human mind is thus deformed is successfully concealed and disguised by laying the blame for the resulting anarchy and confusion *on the human mind itself*, on ' human nature,' on 'the fallibility of human reason.' The intrinsic constitution of man is made the scapegoat for the psychological effects of the constitution of the social organism. That is, of course, an utter misrepresentation. Those deformities, those imbecilities, those absurdities and perversities, are not the product of ' human nature ' at all, but of the predatory social organism that transmits them. They are handed down from generation to generation in the human mind, by its social heredity, not by its psychic or physiological heredity.

A new psychological *fixation*, similar in its result, though different in its operation, from that produced by instinct

14

in insects, is brought about by the social transmission of
' custom,' ' tradition,' ' authority,' and their falsification
in the interests of power. And the same contest is renewed
between the arresting, stabilizing forces of feeling—here
represented by the ' values ' of power interests—and the
labile and developmental forces of cognition, between the
fixed and transmitted values of artificial æsthetic reaction,
and the values of the individual freedom of noetic reaction
—' judging for itself.' Human evolution has taken place
by the operation of the latter in spite of the gigantic
handicap. But in bringing about that evolution those
cognitive powers, universally decried and denounced as
being opposed to ' right feeling ' and congenitally imbecile,
have operated in a curiously indirect manner. They have
never operated directly, with purposive evolutionary ends
in view, constructively, but by criticism, destructively ;
by sapping and invalidating those falsifications upon
which dominating powers are founded. Here as elsewhere
the forces of development have proceeded unconsciously,
the purposes of Life have been carried out ' blindly ';
even though its instrument has been the most highly
developed form of conscious power and purpose, of
directed thought.

The most striking manifestation of that process is
presented by that aspect of human development which is
known as the moral aspect. It is, as we have seen, the
process of adaptation of the individual to the social
organism, and as such is one of the chief tasks with
which the forces of life are concerned in human development. That ethical aspect has occupied an enormous
place in human thought, which is replete with moral
values, and ethical ideas, which has constructed ethical
systems, and been fired with ethical enthusiasms. But all
that ethical thought has been virtually of no account as
a factor in the actual process of ethical development. And,
strangest fact of all, what measure of influence it has
exercised over the development has been directed *against*

it. Ethical evolution has taken place apart from ethical thought, by opposition to domination, by the gradual destruction of the falsifications of power-thought, by critical thought undirected to any ethical ends. It has taken place, not through the advocates of 'goodness,' but through the advocates of ' wickedness '; not through the saint, but through the rebel.

The human mind, which in all its peculiarly *human* elements is a social product, is thus superposed upon the vital foundation of natural impulses and values, as an artificial superstructure raised tier upon tier—by the symbolism of language, by the social transmission and transformation of all concepts and values—above the realities of existence. The human focal consciousness, the most sharply defined form of consciousness, is thus at the same time that from which the motive forces of life are most darkly hidden, in which they are most *unconscious.* Hence that profound impression of ' artificiality,' of unreality, which life makes upon us.

Our whole daily procedure is ruled by super-physiological, by superorganic instincts more blindly fixed in dead mechanism than the structural psychological stereotype of the insect. We rise at the call of a customary time-table, dress and breakfast at the behest of the clock, the cog-wheels of which have become our masters and the regulators of our organic appetites. We attend to our avocations, the common round, the daily task. Our work is performed according to the set rules of the game ; our intercourse with our fellows, formal or intimate, follows specified customary formulas and conventions. We make love according to book. Our pleasures and recreations are no less than our ' duties ' confined within the frame of current prescriptions. Our life-work, be it the most mechanical drudgery or the most skilled brain-labour, is the observance of set rules. In our most creative work itself ' public opinion,' the critics, the conventional formulas, are ever at our elbow ; could we wholly forget and disregard them, we should become unintelligible. At the climacterics and cross-roads of our lives we decide our fate with the same narcotic conformity as we choose the colour of our neck-gear. Do we not, when perplexed, even seek *advice*—so as to ensure ourselves against any danger of originality ?

On how many occasions have the psychical forces within us, the daring appetites, the infinite possibilities of the life-force, the honesties of thought, the royal ideo-motor powers of control, been thoroughly aroused and on their mettle ? How often have we been really wide awake ? —*we*, the fundamental forces and powers in our being ? How often have they been called upon to act, to manifest themselves, moved to decide in accordance with what we know, what we actually believe ? How often has our soul been creative ?

The nature of ' genius ' is debated in unlearned societies with considerable drollery. In the midst of a world fettered in the toils of transmitted thought, custom, tradition, and orthodox values, there appears a man that spontaneously thinks and acts, that is in mind and action creative. He is gaped at with hostile indignation mostly, and, mayhap, hoisted after his death upon an altar and canonically pronounced to belong to the species ' genius.' His valet, however, that is, your valet-minded friend, will tell you that he knew Mr. Hero-Genius quite well, and that he was a person much like any other, who really ate and smoked like you and I ; a person, if the truth be told, somewhat disappointing, of poor and at times incoherent conversation, decidedly rude and mannerless, and in much of life's commerce singularly helpless ; a person with vices too ; on the whole a much overrated person.

Nothing is more rejoicing than our current gibberings, and even our profoundest pronouncements, concerning genius. Ask what a man of genius is, and you will be told that he is a superior kind of man, a great man, a sort of superman, as it were. Or more humorously still you will be informed in tones of subtle penetration that ' genius is an infinite capacity for taking pains.' Sir Francis Galton even more strangely bestows upon the world a treatise, accounted a classic, imparting the surprising information that genius is ' hereditary,' and disclosing the fact that the Pitts and the Scaligers were geniuses ; and that, in short, Sir Francis has not the remotest notion of the meaning of the word ' genius ' beyond what he has gathered from Johnson's Dictionary.

Talent, ability, capacity for taking pains, belong to a psychological rubric only remotely and incidentally connected with the rubric *Genius*. In order to have genius you must have originality. Originality—that is, not the mere freakishness of intentionally whimsicality, but the breaking away of your soul from the bonds of custom-thought and falsified power-thought, and the achievement of its freedom. The play of human power in liberty from that bondage is what in art, in science, in literature, in politics, in practical engineering, in thought, in conduct, constitutes the quality of genius. If to that quality you have also superadded talent, ability, then you have the realization of genius.

There are of necessity under the life of standardized thought and behaviour, dark, simmering depths. Beneath the routine of a well-behaved, conforming life a score of ' we's,' as unlike that ' faultlessly ' dressed diner and his table manners as a corroboreeing black-fellow, lie draped, suppressed, and partly asphyxiated. We flick the ash of our cigarette and keep up the conversation over our coffee, apparently respectable enough and safe personages. But under that unexceptional attitude and manner there stirs somewhere a roaring wild beast, a howling naked savage, an Eliogabalus ; and likewise too, maybe, a hero, a martyr, an unbrowbeaten thinker, a perished artist, as shy of issuing out of their darkness, their conventional cell, as the brute and the troglodyte.

Yet they are there, primal appetites, immense aspirations and all, really and actually alive in us.

What in that orderly life of routine becomes of them, the unacknowledged, unknown doubles that shadow the well-behaved, law-abiding, opinion-abiding citizen ?

They may on occasion burst forth with terrible, astonishing effect ; the platitudinarian gentleman may actually be revealed to us transformed into a raving, wallowing, brute-beast. Or he may become transfigured into a sublime hero. That happens on occasions on the whole exceptional. On occasions not exceptional they nevertheless do express themselves, find some vent of expression for themselves in some manner or other.

They express themselves in the first place by pronouncing the routine of life a terrible boredom, by making us feel their unutterable tedium. They will at times drive us to go to sea, to the South Pole, to Western Uganda, to Northern Thibet, ' in search of adventure.' If war breaks out we pronounce it an appalling calamity, and assume our most solemn countenance, but the savage and the hero within us are up and rejoicing ; they have their opportunity, they will obtain their freedom. Our bored, enchained savages crave for 'excitement.' Our fascinating Lady Frippery is—everything that she should be ; but she must at all cost have excitement. That is what the bored, virtuous savage calls for from the depths.

It is in those activities that are farthest removed and most immune from the influence of the social strife and its falsifications, in non-utilitarian, *useless* activities, in our amusements, pleasures, tastes, fictions and daydreams, that the psychic realities within us come to light and expression. The essential information concerning people in *Who's Who* is to be found under the rubric *Recreations*. The superior importance of those activities is proclaimed by the vulgar evaluation of our commercialism in the very disparagement which it casts upon them ; for, being ' useless,' they are ends in themselves, possess an intrinsic worth for their own sakes, and are not, like the activities imposed by the panic of necessity, mere means to *other* ends. Artistic values, then, are the significant expressional and revelatory values. For in its essential significance, art is not what you go out to inspect in galleries and exhibitions ; it is not what supplies the theme of art-talk. That is but a narrow aspect of the thing which, psychologically, is as wide as life, which is part of every act and gesture. Your affective self, your inmost self, expresses itself in every act ; the very bodily features of a man, his facies, corporeal twitchings, and methods of ambulation, are stamped no less sharply than his motives and ideals, and for the same reason, with the values ' high,' ' low,' ' noble,' ' ignoble,' and assign to him his place in the scale of evolution, of evaluation. In all he does his self is to a greater or less extent indelibly prefigured ; but most clearly in what he does ' for its own sake,' under no dictation but that of his impulses and instincts, likes and dislikes. That is why art is psychologically so important ; why carved stones and painted potsherds are humanly significant and interesting.

Art, as the creative expression of those deeper values which no mere discursive, ratiocinative language, untouched with emotion, can convey, is not essentially noble or beautiful. Its merit, as art, is conditioned by the skill of mastery over the means of expression, and by the truth, that is, the sincerity and spontaneity, of that expression. Qualities which are of necessity conflicting ; for conscious skill inevitably checks spontaneity : hence the charm of the unskilled 'primitive,' in whom technique has not killed the superior worth of spontaneity of expression. But, however faithful or skilful the expression, the ultimate worth must needs lie in the mentality that is expressed. Art, in every sense, is the expression of man's place in the scale of life, of life's development, of his nobility or of his baseness. It is the expression of human sottishness no less than of human divinity.

The horrors of our coloured-cover literature, of our pornographic music, of our genteel architecture, fall under the rubric *Art*. They are the art of our mentality, expressive, representative of it. Art can be that, or it can be Parthenons and Symphonies Pathétiques, according to the soul of which it is the expression.

Hence the abiding medicinable redeeming virtue of all great art, of the expression of the soul of the past in periods of less disturbed health, of more settled world-outlook. Yet no expression of the past can serve truly for that of the present. The affective values and realities of life depend upon its cognitive outlook and must needs change with it. No art, no emotional expression, however great, whose cognitive values are no longer true, can nurture us truly, however much they may heal and cleanse us. To take up our abode there, is to fall out from the march of life, to withdraw from our age and its evolution, to become reactionaries. To us who stand as ' on a peak in Darien' before new horizons, no great art is possible, because we live amid values that are ' no more ' and values that are ' not yet.' In the convulsion of a world over-taken at last and overwhelmed by the Nemesis of the accumulated falsifications and mendacities of its heritage the true expression of our souls' realities, in the battle-glow of the hour, cannot be other than one of strife, of revolt. And strife, however noble its aim or beneficent its fruits, is always in itself ignoble, *debasing*. Strife calls for the defensive attitude, the operation of the instincts of self-preservation ; and those instincts, subsidiary and instrumental merely, as a necessary evil, to their opposites, to the extra-individual impersonal impulses, are the source of all vicious, base, ungenerous tendencies in life. The baseness, the sterility, of the present times, are the outcome of the hypertrophied self-defensive, self-preserving impulses, of the fear, the caution, the suspicion, the egoism which strife, conflict, engender. Our ' materialism,' our vulgarity, our incapacity for great art, are the effect of that.

CHAPTER X

THE ILLUSION OF INDIVIDUALITY

THE whole edifice of human conceptions has been built, ultimately, upon a single concept—that of individuality. The philosopher, who in his analysis takes down the edifice stone by stone, comes at last upon the foundation-stone, proclaims his discovery—' *Cogito, ergo sum* '—as the bedrock of all certainty, and proceeds to rebuild upon the self-same foundation. Religion likewise rests upon the concept of the individual ' soul '; and the task of academic psychology is to protect it and its various aliases—the ' Ego,' the ' experient,' ' the subject of psychology,' ' the transcendental unity of apperception,' —against corrosive analysis. Human life, emotional, social, political life, proceed upon the same fundamental postulate, and are concerned with the ' individual,' with ' individuals,' and with nothing else. The forces of Life and the realities of the Universe proceed on their courses utterly incognizant of ' the individual ' and without any consideration whatever for our fundamental concept ; to our profound distress and pained perplexity.

There are gross, obvious grounds for the conception. You perceive yourself by reflection as a coherent thing persisting amid various settings, delimitated from an external world by a surface of skin. The domain of your feelings extends to that surface ; your fingers and your toes feel, your umbrella and your shoes do not. Outside the frontier of your skin lies an external universe which is not-you. A metaphysician comes along and sorely perplexes you by pointing out that your skin-bound body and that external universe are, for ought you can show to the contrary, but parts of your own mind, that all you know of them are feelings and sensations of your mind, and nothing more. That staggering demonstration, against which you are powerless to urge anything relevant, makes not the slightest difference. Let the solipsist have his way, let Sirius and Altaïr, the metaphysician and your umbrella, let your sensient skin-bag be ideas in that world of your mind. That world ' of your mind ' is still exactly the same world divided into two by the surface of your skin.

You are not only coherent in space, you are also continuous in time. That coherent system which is reading this page is, so far as respects continuity in time, the same system as the child who once laboriously spelled c-a-t, cat.

Like every coherent system, you have your own peculiar characteristics. No two pebbles on the beach are exactly alike, and you differ in several ways from everybody else. But that does not constitute your ' Ego ' any more than the coherence, continuity, and discreet peculiarities of the pebble constitute a pebble-ego.

If the views which have been expressed in the foregoing pages are correct, substantial support may be offered to the Ego-conception from the consideration that the whole diversity of feelings, thoughts, and actions are manifestations of a common original conative disposition which is the source of them all, and is the same throughout the sentient organism. But that is equally true of the pebble. The disposition of energy in the pebble causes it to react in a determinate way to determinate conditions. In the pebble those reactions are fixed and unmodifiable, whereas in the living organism the disposition which is manifested in its reactions is modified by every one of those reactions, so that it is always changing. If you call your conative disposition your Ego, that is then a much less permanent and stable thing than the pebble individuality.

'But,' says the traditional psychologist, 'since you think, since you feel, since you do things, there must be a thinker, a feeler, a doer.' That is the grand argument of traditional psychology. Here we have the ' subject ' of psychology. Before considering it let us, if you please, first consider the pebble as a doer.

Exactly ·the same thought-puzzle arises in connection with our pebble.

All the reactions, the ' properties ' of the pebble have been resolved by the investigations of physical science into ' modes of motion.' Until quite lately one 'property ' remained which was not resolvable into motion, and which accordingly served as a measure of the quantity of matter. " Metaphysicians," said Clerk-Maxwell, " have failed to perceive that the sole unalterable property of matter is mass. Even to this day those who are not familiar with the free motion of large masses, though they admit the truth of dynamical principles, yet feel no repugnance in accepting the theory known as Boscovitch's that substances are composed of systems of points which are mere centres of forces. . . . It is probable that many qualities of bodies might be explained on this supposition, but no arrangement of centres of force, however complicated, could account for the fact that a body has a certain measurable mass. No part of the mass can be due to the existence of the supposed centre of force." There is some piquancy in the circumstance that the answer to Clerk-Maxwell came not from any misguided metaphysician, but from Clerk-Maxwell's own successor at the Cavendish Laboratory in Cambridge, where the above words were written. He dispelled that last residual ' property ' of matter and showed it to be an exponential function of motion. Motion of what ? Here we are brought back by our pebble to precisely the same situation as that which gave rise to our ' subject of psychology.'

If there is motion, there must be something that moves ; to speak of motion without something moving is not grammatical. That, of course, is so—as a matter of grammar. Our concept of motion embodied in our grammar refers to the motion of coherent systems ; but when we have resolved the whole of those coherent systems into their elements the concept of motion fails us : we are left with a verb without a subject.

In demanding a subject for our verb we are asking for the 'cause' of the motion. When we have got down to motion without anything being left to move, we have got beyond motion in the form of our experience to the ' cause ' of motion. And the ' cause ' here, as we have seen, is not at all the 'agent,' but that of which the sense presentation is the *sign*. In our motion without anything moving what we need is not a subject for our verb, but a thing of which motion is significant. That thing is what physicists call energy, a thing which, as we cannot conceive it or describe it by its causes, we are compelled to describe by its effects—as that of which motion is significant. ' Motion ' is for us the motion of coherent systems, of things formed, upon which we can act by altering that form. If that were anything more than a symbolic, schematic representation of our possible action, our grammatical logic would hold good to the end ; but when we have analysed down the system, and completely resolved its configuration, what is left is no longer ' something that we can act upon,' something the form of which we can alter—since there is no form left to be altered ; our symbolic concept of 'matter and motion,' and our grammatical logic are no longer applicable. We have passed out of the sphere of possible action, and the ' motion without anything moving ' is no longer our symbolic representation of ' matter and motion,' but that for which the symbol stands, the ' cause of motion.'

The ' doer,' the ' thinker,' stand in exactly the same predicament as the ' moving thing.' They are applicable concepts so long as we deal with the complex, coherent system as we have it. But resolve those systems into their components, and they both vanish. Just as the concept ' motion ' is only applicable to a formed coherent system which we can act upon, so the concepts ' thinker,' ' doer,' are only applicable to the formed and coherent systems which we call ' we.' The thinker of the thoughts is that coherent whole just as the object of the ' properties ' of the stone is the stone. Analyse the stone down, the object vanishes ; analyse the thinker down, the subject vanishes. There is a relation of subject and object in each of our cognitive acts—sensations, concepts, thoughts ; but those cognitive acts are only possible to an elaborately formed system or disposition, and the subject is not otherwise discoverable than as that coherent and continuous aggregate of which our sensations, concepts, thoughts, are manifestations. As soon as you *analyse* it, as you take the configuration to pieces, there is no subject left.

So that for the grounds of our conception of the subject we are thrown back, after all, on those manifest and unsophisticated facts of coherence and continuity from which we started. Psycho-metaphysical analysis of the ' *cogito* ' adds nothing to those manifest facts ; and if we would study further the nature of the cogitant, it is by turning our attention to the nature of that coherence and continuity that we must do so, and not by postulating grammatical subjects for our verbs. Here again the most satisfactory knowledge available to us is knowledge of origins ; ' scire ' is not ' per causas scire,' but ' per origines scire.'

That coherent organism which we call our ' self ' is not something which at a given time became created out of nothing and entered the universe. It has developed from a cell, the product of the fusion of two germ-cells, that is, cells functionally unspecialized and undifferentiated, in which the conative dispositions of two other organisms were present. They accordingly reproduced the reactions of the parent organisms, beginning from the stage when those organisms were also functionally undifferentiated cells, and passing through all the steps of their differentiation in mutual relation to each other, to the building up of a differentiated aggregate of complex configuration, its development, growth, ageing, decay and death. In the course of that process—the individual life—the common conative dispositions of the new organism become modified, and those modifications of all its constituent cells are necessarily transmitted to another generation. That process is continuous, and has been repeated from the first beginnings of life. The individual life is only one step, one link, one phase, in the process. There is no break in it. There is as much continuity between the phases which we call generations of individual lives as between those which we call childhood, maturity, old age. The ' thing,' the continuous and coherent system, is not the individual, but the entire chain of life. Life develops, the individual develops ; the one development is part of the other. The abstraction of the particular phase, ' individual,' out of the continuous series is as purely arbitrary, a mere convenient abstraction, as if we were to choose a period of a day, or of a century, or of a thousand years, as our unit. The ' individual ' is an artificial unit. The circumstance that there is a break in cognitive consciousness between one generation and another, that your ' memory ' does not reach beyond the cycle of your individual life—it does not even cover the whole of that—and that cognition is not transmitted, is a very superficial and irrelevant consideration. A great deal besides is cognitively unrepresented in our consciousness ; the very forces that determine the operation of that consciousness are not cognitively represented in it.

Those are, like our organism, the product of the whole chain of life. In precisely the same way as your reactions, your feelings, are related to one another,

thus giving rise to your ' unity of apperception,' making
your experience into a coherent whole, an ' individual '
experience, so are they also related to, and bound up
with, the reactions, the feelings, of primordial protozoa,
of organisms, in which life has developed those reactive
tendencies, those feelings, those appetites, those sentiments,
those modes of cognition which operate in you, and constitute your active psychism. Your mental attitude at
this moment is as intimately related to the reactions of
life in some primordial marine creature as they are to
the impressions of your childhood and of your youth.
The only line of demarcation between you and the
continuity of Life is that of your cognitive experience.
And to make that an essential and fundamental
demarcation is a purely cognitive, intellectualistic interpretation.

You live in a cognitive world of word-symbols, you
think—that is the foundation of your *ergo sum*! But
that thought-world, which illusively appears to constitute your psychic life is but its thin superficial vesture.
Its folds are moulded by a throbbing form of appetences,
of yearnings, which the world's contacts thrill into feelings.
Your thought-world is but an appanage of that pulsing
reality, the waves of which reach back to the distant
horizons of a strange past and move towards unknown
futures far beyond the phase of your ' individual ' life.

That thought-world—do you believe *that* to be ' you ' ?
Has it not been manufactured for you in human workshops
as have your clothes and the furniture of your house ?
How much of that ' you ' would exist, I ask again, had
you been marooned in a desert island and providentially
enabled to live there at all ? Your concepts, your thoughts,
your views and opinions, and firm beliefs, how each
experience and event of life ' strikes you '—to trace those
is not a matter of metaphysical, or even of biological,
investigation, but merely of human history. Your concepts are arranged alphabetically in any dictionary.

The mountain-mass of prejudices by means of which you judge, praise, condemn, and wax enthusiastic or indignant, have been handed to you by all sorts of queer-looking persons wearing antiquated clothes—and also by the Fleet Street paper which you read this morning at breakfast.

But you actually dare to ' think for yourself,' you have actually uprooted some of those prejudices from your mind, torn the stones from the walls of your prison ; you have asserted your 'individuality.' Brave deed ! After those stones had been thoroughly loosened for you by the imperceptible efforts of whole armies of thinkers ; after every grain of cement had been slowly corroded from around them, and the crowbars of generations had tugged at them, you have actually managed to lift the stone out and cast it from you, and you proudly exclaim, ' Behold what *I* have done ! ' Your cogitative, cognitive life is, like all the other ingredients of your life, *part of a process*, which extends far, very far, beyond you, of which your thoughts—supposing you to be the deepest and acutest thinker of your age—are but one small constituent element. Imagine a secluded colonial settlement entirely cut off from human civilization, and composed of Shakespeares, Newtons, Darwins, with a few Nietzsches thrown in ; you might expect in vain plays, Principia, Theories of Evolution, or Transvaluations of all Values, to issue thence.

That cogitative world, that world which constitutes the largest bulk of our focal consciousness, of our ' *cogito*,' is certainly of all aspects of our organism that which has least claim to any individuality. It is a social product ; the most superficial, extraneous, negociable, delusional, gullible portion of our ' selves.' It is the material upon which the public newspapers and every species of quack operates contentedly, ' moulding public opinion.'

It is *in spite of* that malleable world of ' *cogito*,' of third-brain concepts and thoughts that, coming to the surface from the dark depths of unconsciousness and inarticulate feeling, and bursting through its artificial film in the form of honesties and realisms, our real sense of individuality, of personality, asserts itself.

What is it exactly that you mean when you say that you propose to affirm, to assert your individuality ? You, in defiance of all conventionalities, ' taking-for-granted,' and sheep-in-the-gap compliances, assert and liberate the inmost impulses which truly actuate you. Surely not *all* ? The police won't let you. Quite apart from the police there are hosts of impulses within you which you do not at all desire to affirm and assert, which, on the contrary, you desire most carefully to conceal and stifle. What you mean when you say that you are going to assert yourself, your individuality, refers to a very carefully selected sample of your individuality. The impulses that desire to assert themselves do so not so much by virtue of their strength as by virtue of their worth. Suppose that you do succeed in ' imposing ' them—how does that come about ? By virtue precisely of that worth, of that importance which impels you to impose them. That self-same quality of your ' individuality ' which urges you to impose it, persuades men to accept it. If that worth be an illusion, you certainly will not succeed in imposing your ' individuality ' in any degree at all. Is it then your ' individuality ' which seeks to impose itself ? Not that at all, but the higher grades and developments, the freer manifestations, of the conative forces that are in you. They impose themselves upon you, and, overflowing, seek to impose themselves upon others likewise. That, then, is the ' individuality' which you deem worth asserting ; not at all the promiscuous impulses, weaknesses, basenesses and ignominies, and miscellaneous instincts that are in you, but those which your evaluating impulse, your sense of value and rank, your evolutionary sense, pronounces to be worth asserting.

It is certainly not in the superficial world of our worded

consciousness, but in those impulses and conative dispositions which are the source of all our reactions, including
that consciousness itself, that we must look, if anywhere,
for the foundations of our individuality.

But those dispositions and impulses, we have already
sufficiently noted, have in their tendency, direction, and
operation, nothing to do with ' us.' It is quite impossible
to maintain that those forces which actuate us are directed
towards promoting our well-being, our ' happiness.' If
there is one clear mark of their general character, it is that
they are utterly unconcerned with promoting the welfare
of the individual. They absolutely disregard it. In no
sense can they be described as individualistic; on the
contrary, they are characterized by the absolute ignoring
of the individual and his interests.

The higher we stand, the more self-development we
achieve, the more we ' assert our individuality,' the less
are our development and assertion individualistic. It is
only on the lower planes, as stunted, warped, arrested,
undeveloped, degenerate misbirths, that we can be
' individualistic,' that our activities can remain within
the sphere of self-preservation and search for ' happiness.'
The human soul does not seek happiness ; only the shop-
keeper soul does that.

All the impulses that actuate us and which rise at all
above the most primitive phase of nutrition or acquisition
are extra-individualistic. Not only do they transcend
individual interests, they are actually antagonistic to those
interests. It is as though they used the individual as
a mere tool, as a mere dupe ruthlessly employed in the
service of interests that are not his, drawn to his own
suffering and destruction by baits that make a fool of
him.

But that view, that mode of expression—that we are
' *used as tools* ' by extraneous forces, by ' Nature '—is
not just or correct. For the simple reason that there is
no ' we ' : there is nothing in us over and above the urging

forces themselves. Those extra-individual, impersonal forces that move us are ' we.' Any conflict arises only between their more developed and their lower forms, between the higher manifestations of those impulses and the more imperfect ones of 'self-preservation' which serve the purpose of maintaining the individual form of life.

To the biologist, as is well known, the concept of 'individuality' has been the source of not a few dilemmas and difficulties. Among the Cœlenterates and Worms the same organic form may at one time lead a separate existence, be an individual, and at another be a part, or organ of a larger aggregate. Among the Siphonophoræ we have the curious spectacle of complete organisms, built on quite different plans of specialization, which would in ordinary circumstances be regarded as different species or different stages in the life-history of a species, existing in organic continuity as a bundle of disparate individuals. Some of the individuals (?) are polyps, others medusæ, some are males, others females, some are palpatory (dactylozooids), others seize prey ; yet all are connected by a common stalk and all act in exact concert. Physalia, for instance, which is such a bundle of diversified 'individuals' which swims in the Mediterranean, accelerates or slows its swimming movements (or rather those of its medusæ 'individuals'), changes its course, turns, dives and plunges, or rises to the surface exactly as if it were a single 'individual.' On the view expressed in the present work the puzzle is elucidated by the fact that where there is organic continuity there is equilibration of all conative tendencies of the organism, no matter how differentiated ; and therefore the anomalous bunch of diverse and disparate organisms, although it has no 'nervous system,' acts precisely as if it were an orthodoxly organized 'individual,' and is in fact an individual. Biological individuality is merely a question of organic continuity, and any agglutinated assemblage of organized living matter can be an ' individual ' provided it can manage to support its life. Any hydroid polyp can be cut with a knife into as many 'individuals' as you may choose, and each fragment will regenerate missing parts and restore itself to the form and organization of a complete polyp. That holds true of plants and of any organism where the specialization of function is not too great ; for the greater that specialization, the less, naturally, is the power of further differentiation, that is, of regeneration and reproduction. Therefore to be capable of reproduction a cell must be functionally undifferentiated. The same, indeed, is strictly true of all organisms, including man. An undifferentiated detached cell—spermatozoon or ovum—leads a separate existence when disjoined from the parent individual and constitutes the starting-point of a new individual life. In a biological sense the concept 'individual' is of quite secondary significance—a matter of subdivision and physical continuity. Individuality can be produced by means of scissors. The 'individual' organism is merely a detached part of another organism.

And, properly speaking, our own sense, feeling, and persuasion of our individuality rests upon that same crude accident of organic discontinuity ; it means that we have no feelings but those of our detached, delimitated organism, and that all the feelings of that quantity of living stuff are 'our' feelings. Our 'individuality' is a share, a measured portion, or slice of the thing, Life. But to regard that slice as something having a fundamental and substantive in-itselfness is plainly the merest inaccuracy. The mere circumstance of its acquired spacial discontinuity is wholly insignificant beside the fact of the actual continuity of its being with the whole of which it is a part. The substantive thing, the actual fact, is not the 'individual,' but Life. It is only as a part of that continuous whole that we, as individuals, exist.

And not of Life only. We must believe—those of us to whom the word-juggles and *deus-ex-machina* contrivances of a superadded ' creation ' are unworthy and unmeaning subterfuges—that the stream of Life had its source in the inorganic world. That stream is, as a verifiable fact, a form, a configuration of the same forces ; it is physically and chemically analysable into the self-same constituents, which it is continually drawing upon and incorporating, and into which it continually reverts. The ' energy ' which is the quantitative measure of its activities is that of the chemical disruption of its molecular systems, that of the combustion of the fuels it consumes, that, ultimately, of the sun. You are, quantitatively regarded, a measured portion of energy which can issue into the displacement of weights by your muscles, the composition of poetry, an act of heroism, or into as much heat as will boil a pot of water. The qualitative differences are manifestations of differences in form, in complexity of configuration. And we can follow in the diversities of configuration in the organic world the waxing tendencies towards that complexity of structural disposition continuously approaching towards those conditions of self-renewal which render the repetition of reaction and its consequent modification possible, that adaptive modification which is the physical counterpart of feeling.

That continuity is apprehensible ; no discontinuity, when we proceed beyond the surface of phenomena, is anywhere discernible. Our dissection of the world into separated and discreet ' objects ' is a purely utilitarian manipulation of our cognition ; an ' object ' is merely such for the convenience of operation of our acts and thoughts upon it ; it is *an aspect of our activity*. We regard the solar system, or the Earth, or a continent, or a mountain, or a stone on that mountain, or an atom in that stone, each as an ' object,' according to our need. Our distinctions and relations are the pattern of our uses which we stamp upon the face of unity. The forms of our spacial demarcations are entirely *functional* ; they have no structural reality. Our ' atom,' for instance, only exists by virtue of its effects upon every other atom in the universe, and is itself but the resultant in a given point *of view*, of all the forces in the universe. The atom and the universe are not separable entities ; our distinction between the one and the other is but an abstractional manipulation.

The same holds good of our distinction between ' us ' and the universe as of all our other distinctions. It is merely contingent on the disposition of our activities, the particular mode of their operation in our consciousness ; it is functional. Those activities and that consciousness are just as much the resultant of the whole universe as the activities of the atom. The *spacial* differentiation between what is inside and what is outside our skin no longer holds in pure thought : the Little World of our elaborated feeling contains the whole of the Big World ; and the Macrocosm which contains the Microcosm is in turn contained within the Microcosm. Our distinctions, demarcations, and relations are here reduced to a juggle of inapplicable categories.

Conception of the Whole, far less ' knowledge,' is not possible ; since all our concepts are of distinctions and comparisons, and the Whole cannot be compared with its parts or with anything else.

A ' scientific conception of the universe ' is an absurdity which is no longer seriously to be broken on the wheel. A scheme in terms of ' matter and motion ' can never be anything else than a mathematical symbol representing our possible molar movements, and can no more ' represent ' the universe than an architect's plans can shelter us from the weather, or the chemical formula of a carbohydrate appease our hunger. If with an ideal completeness of knowledge, infinitely fuller than our present knowledge, we knew the structure and configuration of the whole universe from the remotest ether-wave to the anatomy of the last atom, we should be scarcely a step more advanced than we are now in our qualitative knowledge of the universe. All that such a symbolic scheme would offer to our contemplation would be a chart of our possible action. Not to elaborate the obvious—does anyone making any claim to common-sense imagine, for instance, that the universe is constructed in view of the range of our telescopic instruments ? If their optical field were the interior of a dewdrop on some gigantic petal, would our science be able to have any suspicion of it ?

Our psychology is no more applicable to the universe than our dynamics. When we have said that the universe is a 'Universal Mind,' what, in fine, does that signify ? It is obvious that thought, sensation, concepts, all forms of cognitive processes whatsoever, which constitute the bulk of our own ' mind,' are wholly inattributable to a Universal Mind ; since there is, *ex vi termini*, nothing outside it to sense or cognize. Thoughts, cognitions, are in our psychology, merely means of giving effect to our impulses, and therefore quite inapplicable to a Universal Mind. Feeling, we have seen, is not attributable to inorganic reactions, since it is the concomitant of modification of reactions, and inorganic reactions can never be modified, for they can never be repeated by the same system. This, it is true, applies only to reactions taken singly and theoretically isolated from the rest of the universe ; and accordingly does not apply to the universe as a whole. But feeling is, like cognition, but a guide to external relations, and therefore meaningless where there are none.

If we have the most elementary understanding of what is meant in our psychology by ' purpose,' can we attach any meaning to the question, ' What is the purpose of the universe ? ' A purpose is with us but a means of steering amid the choice of ways ; it belongs, as much as our cognition and our thought, to the instruments and methods employed in the narrow conditions of our specific activity. It is the distinctive characteristic of all the reactions of the inorganic universe that no trace of ' purpose' is ever discoverable in any of them. But when we are led by the argument from complete absence of design in nature to call the universe ' purposeless ' our predicate is as meaningless and inapplicable as our demand for a ' purpose.' The tendency, the direction which every activity implies, wholly transcends our category of finality.

The application of those terms to the universe does not assist us in assimilating it to our psychological experience. Neither from our physical nor from our psychological forms can we derive any concept of the universe.

Far less than either are our *ethical* values applicable. These are the effect of circumstances and relations altogether peculiar to human development, and are therefore even more limited in their application than the forms of our experience. They cease to have any meaning beyond the sphere of those social activities and relations which are the medium of human evolution. If they were, as has been so persistently imagined, applicable to the universe we should be under the necessity of regarding it as the manifestation of an infinitely malignant power. From the moment that we attempt to transfer those values to the universe we behold it as a nightmare of callous and refined cruelty. On its brow is written, as on that of the Spirit of Evil, that it ' never loved any soul.' [1] The beauty, grandeur, majesty of the aspects of the universe—we hardly need a psychologist to tell us—are not, like artistic values, expressions of qualities in the creative forces that produce them, but of our own moods and affections. That majestic cloud vision is ready to strike us dead ; those calm snow-peaks that exalt our spirit are ready to dash us to pieces and to bury us in their avalanches with as much indifference as

[1] Man sieht, dass er an nichts keinen Anteil nimmt,
Es steht ihm an der Stirn geschrieben,
Dass er nicht mag eine Seele lieben.
Faust.

they would the boulders of their moraines; that siren isle-studded southern bay that thrills us with its intoxicating loveliness is a death-trap which swallows up entire populations in its earthquakes and overwhelms whole cities under its streams of fire; that sea is the emblem of treacherous inconceivable cruelty. Hear what a seaman, a great poet and lover of the sea, has to say of that aspect of Nature which may fairly be taken as representative of her grandeur and majestic power: " He—man or people—who, putting his trust in the friendship of the sea, neglects the strength and cunning of his right hand, is a fool! As if it were too great, too mighty for common virtue, the ocean has no compassion, no faith, no law, no memory. Impenetrable and heartless, the sea has given nothing of itself to the suitors for its precarious favours. The sea—the truth must be confessed—has no generosity. The most amazing wonder of the deep is its unfathomable cruelty." He goes on to relate the rescue of the survivors from a water-logged ship one morning when " the peace of the enchanting forenoon was so profound, so untroubled that it seemed that every word pronounced loudly on deck would penetrate to the very heart of the infinite mystery born of the conjunction of water and sky. On that exquisite day of gently breathing peace and veiled sunshine perished my romantic love to what men's imagination had proclaimed the most august aspect of Nature. The cynical indifference of the sea to the merits of human suffering and courage revolted me. And I looked upon the true sea—the sea that plays with men till their hearts are broken, and wears stout ships to death. To love it is not well. It knows no bond of plighted troth, no fidelity to misfortune, to long companionship, to long devotion." [1]

But to ascribe cruelty, callousness, malignity, to the universe is, of course, a misconception as absurd as to ascribe to it ' love,' ' goodness,' ' compassion.' The one

[1] Joseph Conrad, *The Mirror of the Sea.*

set of values is as inapplicable as is the other; for
they are values of our social-commerce morality, of our
inter-individual morality, and have nothing to do with
our relation to the universe or its relation to us. To apply
those values to the universe leads us, like all absurdities
of thought, into an antinomy : If the universe be
evil, how come we, who are issued from it, to judge it
to be evil ? If the universe were the handiwork of
a malignant God, we should have to forgive God—for
Man's sake.

The morality which is entirely absent from the universe
is the individual-morality, the respect of persons, the love,
kindness, compassion, justice,—the morality which has
reference to the relations between individuals. Of that
the universe shows no trace or symptom ;—is it to be
expected that the adjustments called for by the con-
tingencies arising out of the constitution of a very special
and peculiar form of organism, the social organism, should
be 'universal laws' ?

The inapplicability of that morality to the universe
nowise excludes a 'morality' from the universe. 'Individual-morality,' which is merely a contingent adaptation
—a *means* again—is not at all our *highest* morality. Our
evolutionary conscience, our intuition of values, is not
greatly concerned with individual welfare—ours or others' ;
it is, in fact, as we have seen, extra-individualistic, impersonal. It refers to quite other values than those of
'individual-morality' ; it is as cruel and unscrupulous as
the universe. And the universal order *does*, as a matter
of fact, take account of, and very ruthlessly punishes,
evolutionary crimes and delinquencies—inadaptations,
unveracities, unpardonable sins against the laws of the
development and growth of Life. Though it does so in
a quite extra-individual manner, punishing 'innocent'
and 'guilty' alike, to the third and fourth generation,
after the fashion of a Hebrew God. The ethics of the
universe according to those higher and real values is

quite another matter than the absurd application to it of the ethical values of our social adjustments.

We are concerned with the individual, and the universe is not. We are concerned with individual values, with the individual's fate ; the universe absolutely ignores everything individual. That, properly speaking, is the root of our misunderstanding of the universe. And that 'individuality' upon which we base our strife-born, power-thought-originated conceptions, is an illusion. That which constitutes the actual *worth* of our 'individuality' consists wholly in its extra-individual, impersonal manifestations. That wherein it is individual-regarding constitutes the baseness and *lower* values of its operation. 'Self-preservation' is the baser instinct necessitated by the use of the individual life as an instrument of impersonal conations. It is a necessary evil, which in all vital and high development is subjugated and suppressed. We call that heroic which sets aside self-preservation. And, with amazing inconsistency, we—our theological sentiments rather—actually have the assurance to suggest that our 'desire for immortality,' that is to say, our expanded instinct for self-preservation, is something noble—' Derives it not from what we have the likest God within the soul ? ' The desire for eternal self-preservation derives from what we have the likest a terror-stricken rabbit within the soul. The eternal self-preservation of our 'individuality' would, when we come to consider it, be a somewhat appalling outlook. The eternal self-preservation of our grocer, our charwoman, and our friend the curate is obviously a prospect to make us weep. Most of the ingredients of our 'individuality' are things of which the eternal self-preservation is not at all desirable, is, on the contrary, highly undesirable.

As for the realities of our 'individuality,' the actual active principles and springs of them, their *primum mobile,* —*those* need no 'self-preservation' : they are of their nature eternal. They do not pertain to our misconception of individuality, they are extra-individual, they are impersonal ; and our distinctions between 'individuals,' between self and not-self, are in the sphere of those realities devoid of meaning and application.

To 'cognize' the universe is not at all an imperative requisite. All that our cognition can avail us—and *that* is no light service—is to restrain us from belittling and desecrating it with the dishonesties of our inapplicable concepts. It is incomputably greater.

What is needful to us is not to cognize the universe, but to know that we can *trust* it—and to rejoice in it. That is the πίστις, the faith that is needful. And is it not established by the fact that the forces that move it and those which actuate us are identical ?

POSTSCRIPT

FIRST AID TO CRITICS

NINE hundred and ninety-nine criticisms out of a thousand on any philosophical evaluation of life proceed from what are currently, and erroneously, accounted two opposed moods, temperaments, or points of view—the rationalistic and the sentimental. There must always be something false in every reply returned from either station to objections advanced from the other, as there must always be something false in the objection ; for the very assumption of the opposed positions is itself a failure to grasp the most elementary and simple relations of the psychological mechanism. It is a manifestation, not of 'temperaments,' but of psychological ignorance. Intellectual processes are 'only' instruments of feeling, but every higher human sentiment has for its object a construction of the intellectual instrument. Hence is every exaltation of human feeling—the whole worth of man—made possible only by that instrument. Even religion rests upon 'evidences,' or, as they were called in lower stages of rational development, 'signs.' Man would have no high sentiments if he had no intellect. To oppose the two is nonsense ; and the only conflict between them is that which I have referred to as the conflict of motives involved in all cognition.

As every product of intellect is true or false, that is to say, produced in the undeflected discharge of its adaptive function or in the perversion of that function when corrupted to bear false and 'agreeable' testimony, so sentiments are true or false according as their objects are legitimate or illegitimate products of the intellect.

The vice of thought called intellectualism or rationalism does not consist in abuse of, or in undue reliance on, the instrument, but in the psychological blunder of mistaking the products of the intellect for an end-in-themselves—as, for instance, in the Platonic Theory of Ideas or the 'scientific' schemes of the universe—instead of recognizing those products for what they psychologically are, objects of sentiment.

The radical, pernicious and fatal misuse of the instruments of cognition, on the other hand, is called mysticism. Mysticism consists in dishonestly filling in the blank cheque offered by a 'mystery.' There are no mysteries—in the sense of blank cheques which we are at liberty to fill in. Every such operation is an intellectual felony. A mystery is a problem that we have not solved, a question to which we have no answer. If that blank in our apprehension is filled in, it ceases to be a blank. But the cheque is invalid ; it is not a legitimate cognitive value, but a forgery. It is a lie, and will sooner or later inevitably get us into appalling trouble.

When the sentimentalist (I am, of course, using the word with no depreciatory connotation) appeals to feeling against the rationalist, the latter retorts, 'Feeling is no instrument of cognition.' When the rationalist appeals to intellect against the sentimentalist, the latter retorts, 'Intellect is but an instrument ; Gefühl ist alles.' Both are right in their retorts ; and both are wrong in the psychological confusion that constitutes their respective attitudes. The sentimentalist who of a product of thought says, 'I feel differently,' is as irrelevant as the mathematician who of a symphony asks, 'What does it prove ? '

The conclusions contained in my last chapter, towards which those of all previous ones converge, will call forth from readers of the most diverse shades of opinion protests at varying heats of indignation. Those conclusions are a challenge to the most fundamental of all notions, to the foundation of all past and current thought and evaluations of life's values, the notion of individuality, the 'sum' that was once regarded as the one solid rock of certainty amid a universe of uncertainties. Berkeley dissolved the 'external world' of the thinker ; I call in question the existence of the thinker himself.

The question raised has, like all others, an intellectual and a sentimental aspect ; but the latter must be kept severely distinct from the former. To approach the problem with the formula 'Individuality is a mystery' is to suborn the competent court and from the outset to prejudice the issue.

The 'mystery'—let us say rather the problem—consists in the double-sided fact that there is an obvious delimitation and segregation constituting the individual, while the delimi-

tating frontiers are no less obviously encroached upon by
the individual's history, and by every one of his 'relations'
actual or cognitive to his 'environment.' The old puzzle
of 'Knowledge'—'How can a thing be known that is not
part of the knower?'—is but one among the violations of
the frontiers of individuality. I go much farther—that
delimitation and self-containedness melt utterly away under
examination. The thinker who claims to point to the essential
is entitled to the credit of not overlooking the obvious. To
thrust the obvious upon him as an objection is the mode of
procedure which was wont to elicit from Nietzsche 'Notes
for donkeys.' Far from ignoring the obvious aspects of
delimitation and segregation which constitute individuality
('in a sense'), I have, I believe, supplied, in the conceptions advanced of organic and inorganic differences, of the
mechanism of feeling, of organic as equivalent to psychological continuity, if not an 'explanation,' at least a mode
of conceiving the delimitation in terms of other knowledge
—which, after all, is the most that any 'explanation' can
do. But that segregation is, admittedly, only one aspect
of the 'mystery' of individuality, which were else no
'mystery.' My challenge does not consist in denying that
qualified and limited aspect, but in affirming that when erected
into the essential aspect of individuality it is superficial and
supremely misleading. But when that superficial and misleading aspect is further promoted to the status of absolute
prototype of 'existence,' it is no longer a merely misleading
error of proportion, but a rank and utter falsehood. There
needs no probing of the concept of 'existence' to condemn
as fantastic its application to a phenomenon which lasts some
threescore years and ten. That is not an existence, but an
event ; it *is* not, it happens. Not only is that segregation
but an 'aspect' of individuality, qualified and contra-
dicted by the ubiquitous encroachments of the 'external
world'; the individual *consists wholly* of those 'encroaching'
forces, and, those abstracted, nothing is left. Historically
and actually the individual is a locus of actuating impulses
which are not limited in time or extension, and which operate
without reference to the individual.

It is with the intellectual product that I have been chiefly
concerned, and not with the development of its sentimental
consequences. I hold, perhaps unwisely, that a thinker
should not do *all* the thinking for his reader ; if the latter is
unable or too lazy to do his share and to develop the proffered

indications, he is scarcely worth the trouble of fuller explicitness. Were I a pragmatist, I should preconise my conclusions on the strength of their affective fruits. The stupendous ascription of substantial existence to the event of individual segregation has been the root of all thought and all religions. What are the fruits ? Dead-sea fruits that have turned the glow of life to dust and ashes, universal mistrust of knowledge, mistrust of all values, mistrust of Life, mistrust of the Universe, the blight of arid futility. It is scarcely an exaggeration to say that the concept of individuality has plunged the world into despair. The apprehension of the truth that individual differentiation is but a superficial and misleading appearance, while the essential fact of existence is, on the contrary, the continuity and impersonal unity of all the forces that represent the substance of being, is the solution of all the problems of sentiment. It invests the values, high, low, base, noble, good and evil, with a meaning. It abolishes the conflict of the individual with an autocratic or patriarchal universe. It robs the conflict of egoism of its polluting obsession. It abolishes the problem of evil ; for the evil against which all existence struggles is its own past, which, being dynamic, it must surpass. It abolishes death, for what does not exist cannot cease to exist, and what is universal cannot die. The infirmities, disabilities and imbecilities that flesh is heir to are the limitations which constitute the pretext for the illusion of individuality ; what we prize in individuality is that which transcends those limitations. What is personal in the individual is base, what is of value is impersonal. The perception of human impersonality is the sign by which man may yet win. It is the giver of that trust and strength, that power and confidence, that fortitude and peace, which thoughts and religions founded on the illusion of individuality have shown that they cannot give.

Printed in Great Britain by
UNWIN BROTHERS, LIMITED, THE GRESHAM PRESS, WOKING AND LONDON

For Product Safety Concerns and Information please contact our EU
representative GPSR@taylorandfrancis.com
Taylor & Francis Verlag GmbH, Kaufingerstraße 24, 80331 München, Germany

www.ingramcontent.com/pod-product-compliance
Lightning Source LLC
Chambersburg PA
CBHW070402270326
41926CB00014B/2671